Moose Dropping and Other Crimes Against Nature

Funny Stories from Alaska

Heres a Goody !

Moose Dropping
and Other Crimes Against Nature

Funny Stories from Alaska

Tom Brennan

Illustrated by Bob Parsons

Epicenter Press

Fairbanks/Seattle

Epicenter Press is a regional press founded in Alaska whose interests include but are not limited to the arts, history, environment, and diverse cultures and lifestyles of the North Pacific and high latitudes. We seek both the traditional and innovative in publishing high-quality nonfiction tradebooks, contemporary art and photography giftbooks, and destination travel guides emphasizing Alaska, Washington, Oregon, and California.

Publisher: Kent Sturgis
Editor: Don Graydon
Cover Design:Elizabeth Watson
Inside Design: Sue Mattson
Cover and inside illustrations: Bob Parsons
Proofreader: Dorene Carel
Printer: Transcontiental Printing

Text © 2000 Tom Brennan
Illustrations © 2000 Bob Parsons
Library of Congress Catalog Card Number: 00-130989

To order MOOSE DROPPING AND OTHER CRIMES AGAINST NATURE, mail $12.95 plus $4.95 for shipping (Washington residents add $1.56 sales tax) to Epicenter Press, Box 82368, Kenmore, WA 98028; visit our website, EpicenterPress.com; or call 800-950-6663.

Booksellers: Retail discounts are available from our trade distributor, Graphic Arts Center Publishing™, Box 10306, Portland, OR 97210.

Second printing April 2002
10 9 8 7 6 5 4 3
PRINTED IN CANADA

A Sneak Preview

The Cold Truth about Alaska

Why Texans have an inferiority complex. Snow- and ice-capades. The real meaning of the double solid line on a curve. And the tragic story of the Alaskan who stopped for a yellow light.

They Do Things Different Up Here

Life and death on the Last Frontier: easy come, easy go. The cheechako and the chainsaw. Shipping pimientos to Barrow. An Alaska outhouse turns the other cheek.

Moose Dropping, and Other Crimes Against Nature

The duck who flew first class. Sleeping with a porcupine. Cat with an attitude. The eagle meets its match. Though the climate is frigid, the walrus stays rigid.

What Time Is the One O'clock Tour?

Where to change your currency to Alaska money. A tourist confronts the oosik. Dave Barry gets to know the people of Alaska (all eighty-five of them).

Where the Blue Yonder Is Truly Wild

Flights of fancy. The embarrassed bush pilot. When an airplane runs out of gas. Archie Ferguson gets some bad advice. How to rescue a naked lady.

Good Government? Good Grief!

The politician with a sense of humor. Jay Hammond lays down the law. The value of asserting inanities in stentorian tones. And a resounding vote for the devil.

Disorder in the Court

America's dumbest criminals. Pieces of pie and other dangerous weapons. The cop who smoked dynamite. Coming home to the jail at Nome. When to let a prisoner have his way.

Humans Versus the Other Animals

Why golfers are crazier than fishermen. The man who wrestled salmon. Reel adventure: fishing in the combat zone. How to stalk the wily field mouse.

Drinking in moderation: a
foreign concept. The only
difference between this bar
and the *Titanic* is that they
had a band. Swill times at
Chilkoot Charlie's.

Hope springs eternal when it comes to fools and their
fortunes. Sawdust Pete starts a rumor. Robert Service re-
veals the strange things done in the midnight sun.

The saga of Soapy Smith. Skagway, where there was more
paint on cheeks and lips than on buildings. Story of the
man who lived on rabbits and sourdough pancakes.

What dogs teach their
people. Susan Butcher takes
a bath. Joe Redington loses
control. The hot dogs of
Iditarod. The retriever that
needed water wings.

Preface

Alaska is a funny place, in every sense of the word. It is at various times weird and wonderful, if not downright bizarre. Being an Alaskan requires many things, not least among them a sense of humor. As a result, Alaska's people often exhibit a goofiness that in lesser climes could be used as proof that the bearers had flipped their lids.

My intent in this book is to provide an insight into the lighter side of life in Alaska as observed by the people who live and work here, as well as by some of its visitors. I cast a wide net to capture enough jokes, personal stories, and anecdotes for a brief cultural journey, a way to experience the Last Frontier in the things that tickle its people. Selections range from the wacky writing on Alaska's bathroom and saloon walls and the puzzling things tourists say, to the malapropisms of former governor Wally Hickel, the linguistic tap-dancing of Congressman Don Young, and the classic North Country poetry of Robert Service.

In researching this book, I was often asked if I had found an Alaskan sense of humor; whether such a thing existed. The answer is yes. Alaskan humor almost always reflects a very real sense of place. Alaskan anecdotes tend toward encounters with bears, moose, and salmon or tales involving sled dogs and floatplanes. Their heroes are the grizzled characters who people this part of the world.

Alaska's vastness and beauty can be overwhelming, its long dark winters difficult to endure. But most Alaskans love the place, and almost all have one unifying characteristic: the ability to laugh—at the weather, the remoteness, the occasional danger, at themselves. Alaska is at the same time the northernmost, westernmost and—because the Aleutian Islands extend across both sides of the international date line—the easternmost part of the United States. That last fact has won many a bar bet, but it has also added to confusion about where Alaska is in the world. But confusion goes with being an Alaskan. Alaskans are inherently directionally impaired; otherwise they would know which way is south and go there.

This book is dedicated to the proposition that humor is alive and well in Alaska. We use the term "well" in its broadest sense, of course, without intending unprovable claims of sound mental health. Judge for yourself; if you find any of the material between these covers to be humorous, you are an Alaskan or have an Alaskan streak in you somewhere. If not—if you finish reading this book feeling as cranky as when you started— you're still not off the hook. Committed cranks fit in Alaska just fine.

Acknowledgments

I would like to thank all those who contributed to this book, both those who volunteered material and those who made the book just by being themselves. The list includes national writers like Garrison Keillor and Dave Barry, Canadians Judith Quinlan and Ruth McCullough; Bob Fink of Alaska and the Yukon, Alaskans like Jay Hammond, Tom Jensen, Lyn Kidder, Elise Patkotak, Joseph Young, Geoff Kennedy, Wayne Anthony Ross, Ben Hilliker, Bill Hopkins, Elaine Atwood, Malcolm Roberts, Bob Bell, Mary Barry, Bob Miller, Joe Rychetnik, Tom Anderson, Norma Goodman, Frank Baker, Patricia Moore, the *Anchorage Daily News*, those who advised me on this novice effort like author Larry Kanuit, my editor Don Graydon, my friend and publisher Kent Sturgis, my sons Peter and Tobin, my wife and infinitely patient companion Marnie Brennan, and above all the people of Alaska, the funniest bunch I know.

Despite moose crossing signs, moose can't read. They do cross the road wherever they please, however.

1 | Bigger Is Better
The Cold Truth about Alaska

Columnist Bill Tobin's description of the weather in Anchorage: "Nine months of winter and three months of pretty darn late in the fall."

TEXAS LOST ITS STANDING as the largest state when Alaska joined the union. The two states have been rivals ever since, with both sides convinced that size does in fact matter.

Take the story of the Alaskan and the Texan who had tipped a few at a tavern in Palmer and were en route home to Anchorage one dark night. Midway across the Matanuska River Bridge, both felt the urge to pee. They got out of the pickup and leaned against the railing, conducting their business under cover of darkness into the river below.

"Ooh, the river is cold," the Texan said, a boastful smile on his face.

"Yeah," the Alaskan countered, "and deep."

Paul Jenkins, an editorial writer for the *Voice of The Times*, was concerned that Alaska's state motto, "North to the Future," had never caught on—and was wimpy compared with that other state's stirring litter-prevention slogan: "Don't Mess with Texas." Jenkins asked readers to suggest a new Alaska motto. Among the nominees:

"Alaska: Where the Mosquitoes Suck and So Does the Legislature."

"The Land of Frozen Fog and Mud."

Jenkins' own suggestion: "Yeah, We Smell Like Fish. So What?"

Even the state's North Slope reserves of natural gas, which contain no odiferous sulfur, got a plug in one proposed motto: "Alaska—Our Gas Don't Stink."

IT'S SO COLD IN ALASKA that the snow just keeps getting deeper and deeper. The kids in Milwaukee are told that if they dig down deep enough, they'll find China. In Anchorage they're told that if they dig down deep enough, they'll find Anchorage.

It's so cold in Alaska that the fire department sends crews around to break frozen dogs away from fire hydrants.

It's so cold in Alaska that lovemaking can be difficult. In January when a couple says they've just broken it off, they could really mean they've just broken it off.

It's so cold in Alaska that if you go outside and don't see your breath, it means one of two things: either it's July, or you're dead. [1]

EARLY IN WORLD WAR II, the commanding officer of a contingent of federal troops in Alaska was trying to decide how much wood his men should cut for their stoves, in preparation for winter.

The commander asked his first sergeant for his opinion. Being from the South, the sergeant could only shake his head. He had no idea how much wood a stove would burn in an Alaska winter.

The commander had an inspiration. "How about asking some of the locals just how bad they think the coming winter is going to be, and stockpile wood accordingly?"

The commander and the sergeant walked the area until they found an elderly Native man sitting in the doorway of his cabin.

"How bad do you think the winter will be?" they asked.

The Native pondered a moment, then said: "It will be a very bad winter."

"How do you know?"

"I see signs," said the old man. "Be very bad winter."

The sergeant pressed the man further. "What signs? Do the beaver have heavier fur? Are the caterpillars fuzzier? What signs?"

The Native shook his head sagely. "No. Much better signs than that."

"What signs?" the sergeant asked.

"I see many white men cutting much wood," the old man replied. "Means very bad winter." [2]

AN ONLY-IN-ALASKA summer weather forecast: "Mostly sunny for the remainder of the night."

THE ALASKA HIGHWAY, also known as the AlCan, runs 1,500 miles from Dawson Creek in British Columbia to Tok, Alaska. It was built during the early days of World War II as a land route for soldiers defending Alaska against an expected Japanese invasion.

Canadian historian Ken Coates described the original road as "OK so long as it didn't rain or snow or stay warm or get cold."

On a visit to Alaska in 1996, humorist Garrison Keillor of *A Prairie Home Companion* recited a poem he says his road crew found on the menu of an AlCan cafe:

Curving in and curving out
and I'm beginning to have my doubt
whether the lout who planned this route
was going to Hell or coming out.

NORTHERN ROAD SIGNS often need some translation for the sake of visitors from the south. Judith Quinlan offers these helpful interpretations:

Speed Limit: A speed limit sign doesn't designate the maximum legal speed. It actually designates the maximum compulsory tailgating speed (MCTS). Below the MCTS, tailgating is compulsory. Above the MCTS, tailgating is, as always, optional.

Bump: The presence or absence of a bump sign bears no relationship to the size of the bump. There are a limited number of bump signs available in the north, and every spring they are moved randomly from one set of bumps to another.

Steep Shoulder: These signs are placed wherever there is no road shoulder and the ditch is a 60-foot cliff with a beaver swamp below—about 90 percent of northern roads.

Soft Shoulder: These signs mean that the road shoulder is made of quicksand, on the edge of a 60-foot cliff with a beaver swamp below—the remaining 10 percent of northern roads.

Moose Crossing: These signs are placed randomly along the highway for the purpose of creating photo opportunities for southerners. Moose can't read, and they cross the road wherever and whenever they please.

No Hunting/No Shooting: These signs are targets, provided for northerners who enjoy shooting holes in signs while driving by at high speed in pickup trucks.

Dotted Line: A dotted line down the center of a highway means tailgate now.

Solid Line: A solid line down the center of a highway means speed up and pass.

Double Solid Line on a Curve Up a Steep Hill: This means that only loaded logging trucks may pass now.

Note about logging trucks: They always have the right of way. Logging trucks do not like to be passed. A loaded logging truck may look, to southern eyes, to be a slow and cumbersome vehicle, but this is deceptive.

All logging trucks have jet propulsion and can accelerate from zero to sixty in six seconds, especially when trying to pass a Honda Civic on a steep hill with a curve and a double solid line. [3]

ALASKA PUT A LAW into effect in 1999 that doubles traffic fines in construction zones. The highway department quickly put up signs saying "Begin Double-Fine Zone" at the approaches to construction sites. But at first there were no corresponding signs at the other end saying "End Double-Fine Zone." Eventually they were added.

A similar injustice has bothered me for years. Along many Alaska highways are signs saying "No Shooting Zone." But you never see one that says "Resume Shooting."

On Tudor Road.

A MOTORIST APPROACHED an Anchorage intersection as the light changed from green to yellow. The motorist came to a stop at the light, surprising the driver of a gravel truck behind him. The massive truck jumped the curb, hit a wall, careened through the intersection, and smashed into a gas station.

The truck driver could hardly feel guilty. He told investigators it was the first time he had ever seen anyone in Anchorage stop for a yellow light.

CONSTRUCTION OF THE TRANS-ALASKA oil pipeline generated an unprecedented economic boom, especially in Anchorage, Fairbanks, and towns along the pipeline corridor between Valdez and Prudhoe Bay. But economic booms have their downside, such as traffic jams, lots of new residents, and some inevitable disgruntlement.

After the first year of the boom, bumper stickers began showing up on cars saying, "Happiness is 10,000 Okies going south with a Texan under each arm." [4]

THE FOLLOWING TALE of disaster and daring in the oil fields was among the writings on the walls of the Bird House bar near Anchorage. As the story goes, a wildcat oil driller hit a gusher on the Kenai Peninsula. Before he could bring the well under control, it spewed a rock that struck a spark and set the gushing oil afire.

The driller saw his entire net worth going up in smoke, so he ordered a famous oil well firefighting crew flown in from Texas. But the fire's heat was so intense the experts could not get within a hundred feet of the wellhead, and the fire burned on.

Finally, in desperation, the driller called on the Soldotna volunteer fire department. The locals came racing out to the site in their little red truck, its bells clanging furiously. They drove within twenty feet of the raging blaze, grabbed their hoses, and contained the fire within minutes.

The driller ran to the fire chief, who stood with his clothes smoldering and helmet melted down around his ears.

"That's the most courageous thing I've ever seen," the driller said. "Here's ten thousand dollars for your volunteer company. I hope you use it to throw yourselves one helluva party."

The fire chief looked wearily at the driller and said, "The first thing we're gonna do is get the brakes fixed on that goddamn truck."

BEAR HUNTER TOM WHITE discovered oil at Katalla on Prince William Sound in 1894 when he fell into a pool of the stuff. He went home, cleaned his gun, and went back to bear hunting. Later he returned to the spot and threw in a lighted match, to see what would happen. The pool went up in a blaze and burned for a week. White wiped away singed eyebrows and resumed hunting.

IGNORANCE ABOUT ALASKA shows up in the strangest places. I stepped out of the shower once to answer a jangling telephone. The call was from a television anchor who wanted to visit the North Slope oil fields. But before the anchor came on the phone, an operator announced dramatically: "This is NBC News in New York. Stand by for a call from the United States."

Beauty is more than skin deep at the annual Fort Yukon
Spring Carnival where contestants must skin a hare.

2 | The Alaska Way
They Do Things Different Up Here

Talk about asking for trouble: An Alaska bank offered a unique premium to new customers purchasing certificates of deposit—an official Iditarod commemorative Smith & Wesson .44-caliber revolver.

IF YOU DON'T BELIEVE that life in Alaska is radically different from those other places, consider the Queen contest in Fort Yukon's Spring Carnival. Contestants participate in the usual talent show, question period, and evening gown competition. Then they must build a fire to melt snow for water, run in a snowshoe race, and skin a hare.

ONE SPRING NOT LONG AGO the mudholes in Homer's unpaved streets became so bad that cars kept getting stuck. They were splashing in and not coming out. At one particularly bad stretch of road, the Alaska Department of Transportation parked a tractor and left the keys in the ignition. Drivers were invited to pull their own cars out of the mud.

A SNOWMACHINE THREW its driver near Selawik, then took off by itself, nobody at the controls, and sped across ten miles of rough country. The local folks rejected the theory of a stuck throttle. They decided the machine was inhabited by an evil spirit and burned it.

A CHEECHAKO (an Alaskan newcomer) charged into the hardware store and cornered the salesman who had sold him his chainsaw.

"I've been trying to cut wood for three days with this thing and it doesn't work worth a damn. I can cut wood faster with a plain old handsaw."

"Let me see it," the salesman said, reaching for the chainsaw. The cheechako followed the salesman into the back room and watched as the man removed the spark plugs and rubbed the contacts with a cloth.

"The plugs look clean as new," the salesman said, then yanked on the saw's starter cord. The chainsaw roared to life.

The cheechako covered his ears with his hands and shouted, "What's that noise?"

BILL TOBIN, editor/columnist for the *Voice of The Times*, visited an Anchorage cardiologist who recommended Bill have a pacemaker installed to improve his heart rhythm. Bill asked the doctor: "How long do the batteries last?"

"Ten years."

Bill, then in his late 60s, commented: "I doubt I'll live another ten years." He expected the cardiologist to say something comforting like "Sure you will."

Instead the doctor said: "In that case, the batteries come with a lifetime guarantee."

JUST AS ALASKANS have a unique way of living and of viewing the world, many are unusual in the way they depart the planet. Some splash themselves across a mountainside in a plane crash, some run a snowmachine through river ice, and others exit in their own highly dramatic manner. A few go in more conventional ways, often in warmer climates.

When Marjorie Bird Cottis, former owner of the popular Stuckagain Heights Dining & Resort in Anchorage, died in Desert Hot Springs, California, in 1999, it was a quiet passing. Her family wrote in her obituary: "She did not even spill the drink she was holding."

NEWSPAPER COLUMNIST Mike Doogan writes about a friend whose first Alaska job was as a government salmon counter. The man later joined a survey crew. "From there," Doogan wrote, "he clawed his way up to road construction. It seemed the sky was the limit; people were whispering he might someday rise to bulldozer driver. But he made a wrong turn somehow and became a journalist. Not every self-made man finishes the job."

For those who work in offices, Doogan offers this fashion tip:

Coats and ties for men, dresses for women, are out, out, out. Proper Alaska office dress is a flannel shirt, oil-stained jeans, and big, clodhopper boots. North of the Alaska Range, an outer layer of lined coveralls is required. In Southeast, of course, the chic outer layer is a yellow, rubber slicker. Men usually complete the ensemble with a greasy bill cap from a heavy equipment company.

A wool shirt can be substituted for flannel. If you are an engineer, you can trade the jeans for khakis. But under no circumstances is a tie allowed in the work-place. And if you wear a coat and tie, your co-workers will assume you're going for a job interview and will be-gin stealing office supplies from your desk. [1]

ALASKANS ARE REALLY BIG on traditions. The federal Bureau of Land Management announced that a program at its Anchorage facility would celebrate the start of Alaska Native Arts and Crafts week. A press release noted that "Dancers wearing kuspuks will perform a welcome, an invitational and perhaps the Pepsi song."

MATTHEW NICOLAI TELLS of growing up in the village of Kwethluk on the Kuskokwim River and joining the Boy Scouts. Among the Scouting requirements was completion of a five-mile hike.

Matthew's mother signed the parental permission slip for the outing but said she couldn't understand what the hike was supposed to prove. Yupik Eskimos routinely walk many miles in pursuit of fish and game—but why would anyone trek five miles and intentionally come back empty-handed?

ANCHORAGE NEWSMAN Geoff Kennedy quotes a

Native leader who spoke about the long-running legal battle over subsistence hunting and fishing. "These days you need two boats," the man said, "one for the moose and one for the lawyers."

WHEN NEWSPAPER COLUMNIST Elise Patkotak arrived in Barrow in 1974, she found life on the Beaufort Sea coast required major adjustments from her previous home in New York City.

For one thing, the supply ship came to Barrow only once a year, when the ice pack moved away from the shore. To keep airfreight costs down, most people ordered supplies a year in advance and had them delivered by the ship. One of Elise's early mistakes was buying a 36-jar case of pimientos—a supply that proved to be more than she could ever use.

Storing a year's supplies in a small house required considerable ingenuity. Elise found, for instance, that stacking soda pop cases and covering them with a colorful cloth created a firm but serviceable couch.

She discovered the downside of her creation when a cold snap froze the cans closest to the floor, causing an explosion and carbonated geyser that sent her guests fleeing.

TOM ANDERSON WAS ASSIGNED to Barrow as an Alaska state trooper in 1963, about the same time as two seemingly unrelated events: installation of a linoleum floor in the trooper's house and organization of a village "honey bucket" pickup service.

One day a cheerful Eskimo gentleman arrived at

Anderson's door to empty the holding tank in the home's chemical toilet. The man entered the bathroom and emerged lugging the filled bucket. When he set foot on the linoleum, his caribou-hide mukluks proved desperately slippery and his feet went out from under him.

The bucket went flying and its contents flooded the floor—believed to be the first indoor sewage spill experienced by a honey bucket service.

WHEN OUR FIRSTBORN SON started getting his teeth, my wife heard that ice cubes wrapped in a face towel would cool the baby's gums and ease the discomfort. It worked. And baby Peter became fascinated with the frozen cubes. He enjoyed zipping the slippery little things around on his high chair and flipping them across the kitchen.

When it came time to show off our new son to Marnie's parents in Massachusetts and mine in Virginia, we headed east, arriving in the middle of a summer heat wave. The grandparents in both places fussed over the baby but worried that the heat was making him fretful.

"Don't worry," Marnie said. "I know just the thing." She went to the refrigerator, filled a soup bowl with ice cubes, and gave it to the baby, who gleefully reached in and began playing.

My sister Mary later told me she had thought that ice cubes were the most natural toys in the world for an Alaska baby. "I assumed that was all he had to play with," she said.

ALASKA HAS A VERY SPECIAL relationship with its

outhouses. Some are elaborately decorated. Some are even mounted on skis and entered in the annual Outhouse Race, a highlight of the Fur Rendezvous celebration in Anchorage.

"Perhaps no institution has contributed more to our democratization and development than this humble structure," writes former governor Jay Hammond in the foreword to a book of photos of these essential facilities. [2]

Caring nothing for the creed, color or social status of those who'd seek solace within its portals, one moment it accommodates the gnarled nates of a trail-toughened bush rat; the next, with equal magnanimity, the billowing buttocks of one to the manor born. . . .

The outhouse invites abuse, forever turning the other cheek, so to speak. No one is denied access (save during prior occupancy) and never does an outhouse seek revenge upon even its most rank defilers. . . .

Like most institutions, with time's passage even the outhouse has not escaped character-corroding modifications.

These make visitations of yesteryear seem all the more heroic: Styrofoam seat covers now often insulate one's nether-parts, and a more parsimonious Sears no longer supplies free toilet tissue. Instead most biffies come equipped with rolls of TP, often in effete pastels. Any wonder we today have not more heroes?

The book of photos by Harry M. Walker features outhouses with stained glass windows and elaborate paint jobs, the biffy with the world's greatest view (Mount McKinley), a john built from half a boat, a throne with carpeted walls, another with hanging flower baskets, a five-seater, and a retired outhouse converted to a liquor store.

THE OWNER OF A gas station decided to liven things up at his remote location by installing a speaker under the floor of his outhouse. He would wait until a customer, preferably female, got comfortably settled in before speaking into the microphone hooked to the speaker: "Excuse me, Madame, I'm working down here!" [3]

A FAIRBANKS MAN once came up with the notion that Alaska would be the perfect place for the nation's new superconducting supercollider, a massively expensive high-tech machine sought by the nation's scientists and about to be funded by Congress. The idea came to him while he was sitting on the toilet.

The Fairbanks community made a serious pitch to locate the machine at the University of Alaska, coming quite close to winning the prize. In the end, Fairbanks was nosed out by a location in Texas and the promoter went back to the bathroom, waiting for his next great idea.

IN 1985 THE STATE OF ALASKA bought the money-losing Matanuska Maid Dairy in order to provide a local market for dairy farmers at Point McKenzie.

Four years later the state put up money to keep a Point McKenzie farm in business so the dairy would continue to have a source of milk.

When production from the farms dropped, the state-owned dairy began trucking milk in from Washington state.

Critics charged that Alaska's state government was becoming vertically integrated, with interests all along the food chain, and would soon be forced to provide more consumers to drink the milk, either through immigration or increasing the birth rate.

ALASKA'S MASSIVE GOOD FRIDAY earthquake of 1964 inspired this effort by Everett G. Gressley of Sterling:

I haven't stopped on my way home since March of sixty-
*   four;*
and blime, I'm not fixin' to be stoppin' any more.
That night I stopped and had a few, shucks it was mostly
*   foam,*
and gettin' on toward supper time, I cut and headed for
*   home.*

My wee one met me at the door and said: "Please hurry,
*   Dad.*
'Tis gettin' on toward supper time, and Mom is pretty
*   mad."*
Says I, "Oh botheration now, the old girl can't scare me."
Says daughter, "Oh ho! Can't she now? Well this I gotta
*   see!"*

I finds a mug and thinks I'll have just one small sip of
*   juice.*
Just as I touched my jug, blime, it seemed all hell broke
*   loose.*
The house went up and stood on end. The cookstove lit
*   on me.*

My jug went flying from my grasp; which way, I couldn't see.

My shoes were gone, my toenails were a-tryin' to comb my hair.
I was tryin' to find the doorway but the darn thing wasn't there.
The Frigidaire was jitterbugging with my wee one's bed.
I tried to grab my wife, but grabbed the neighbor's wife instead.
I patted her a wee bit and said: "Honey, don't you cry."
"I'll honey you," says she to me, and poked me in the eye.

In my garage I had some cans and bottles in a sack.
They clanged and rattled 'til a million chills ran up my back.
I thought of all the times I'd stopped at that greengrocery store
and made a solemn vow I wouldn't do it anymore.

My little dog was frightened, fair to blowing out a fuse.
The cat was squalling like she only had one life to lose.
Out went the lights! Out went the stove! No juice, no lights, no heat.
I told my wife: "I've had enough. Now stop it and let's eat!"

About this time, goodbye garage! And with it went both cars.

Above my head I noticed there was nothing but the stars.
'Twas then I promised my good wife, if she would only
   stop,
I'd come straight home from work each night and never
   touch a drop. [4]

How high are the moose taken at the Talkeetna Moose Dropping Festival, animal rights activists wanted to know.

3 | Wild Life

Moose Dropping,
and Other Crimes Against Nature

A tourist asked: "What is the best month to see the whales mate?" A bystander mumbled that Alaska whales do it like real Alaskans: "In Hawaii in January."

EACH YEAR THE PEOPLE of Talkeetna hold a Moose Dropping Festival—named, believe it or not, for the material that moose drop behind them as they go about their daily business. Animal rights activists once demanded more information. How high are the moose taken, they wanted to know, before they are dropped? The activists were ready to sue.

The festival is one of several annual Alaska events in which moose droppings play a central role. In another, an Anchorage Rotary Club raises money by selling numbers that are painted on dried moose droppings, known as moose nuggets. The numbered nuggets are then released from a helicopter onto a ground target. The person holding the number on the nugget that lands closest to the center of the target wins the money.

CANADIAN NATURALIST Angus Gavin got a call one day from oil workers at Prudhoe Bay. They had a question for this environmental consultant to the Alaska oil industry.

A late-migrating duck had flown into the side of a building and knocked itself unconscious, they told Gavin. They found the bird lying in the snow and brought it inside, where they warmed and fed it.

The consensus among those on the scene was that the animal must have lingered too long, missing the migration, and was in danger of freezing to death. So they turned the duck over to an Alaska Airlines flight attendant, who promised to take it to Seattle and release it there. The oil workers had called Angus because they wanted to know—after the fact—if they had done the right thing.

Gavin asked what the duck looked like. Upon hearing the description, he responded in his distinctive Scottish burr: "Well, the trip probably won't hurt it, but that duck wasn't going to Seattle. They winter in the Aleutian Islands."

MANY PEOPLE TELL of waking up to find a porcupine in bed with them. This usually means the guy needs a shave or the woman is exhibiting a prickly temperament. But for Kenny Baker, a Seward gold miner in the 1940s, the meaning was literal.

Camping under a canvas lean-to, he awoke one crisp fall morning to the feeling that something was pushing against his side. Baker turned over cautiously and saw a porcupine snuggled up to his sleeping bag, fast asleep, enjoying the warmth from his body.

He knew that making a sudden movement was probably a bad idea. He tried coughing, making noise, and moving slowly in his sleeping bag, but the porcupine just snuggled closer. Finally he decided to make a break for it by simply rolling quickly to the side. The porcupine woke up, looked distraught, and padded off into the woods. [1]

ANCHORAGE IS ALASKA'S largest city, but it also has its wild animals, and they're not all humans. This transmission was overheard on a police radio scanner:
Officer 1: "I'm going out on a moose call."
Officer 2: "How many bullets do you have?"
Officer 1: "About four or five hundred."
Officer 2: "That ought to do it."

"EVEN A MOOSE is subject to the law of the land," writes author Dermot Cole, who goes on to say:
At least that's what the Fairbanks mayor and city council decided in 1913 when a bartender's pet moose became too much of a bother. The ordinance gained such notoriety that you can still find books that claim Fairbanks is the only place in the world where it is against the law for a moose to use city sidewalks

Pete Buckholtz, a bartender in Bill McPhee's saloon . . . had acquired a calf moose from hunters. "The animal became very tame and would follow either Pete or me," Charles Schiek recalled.

"The moose had been broken to harness and could be hitched to a sled. In winter he was fed on potatoes and stale bread and sometimes either Pete or I would go into the woods, then nearby, and cut some willow for the creature. I remember he wouldn't eat rolled oats."

The moose had "gained in docility and affection" when Mayor Andrew Nerland decided that something had to be done. The moose followed Buckholtz and, like him, made its headquarters in McPhee's saloon. Buckholtz had been asked many times to keep the moose out of the saloon, but he refused.

City officials could not prohibit possession of a live moose, but there was a city sidewalk in front of the saloon and the city fathers could ban moose from city sidewalks. The moose was the only one in Fairbanks and the ordinance was designed to keep him out of the saloon.

The Associated Press distributed the moose tale, and it continues to be mentioned today by writers who mistakenly assume that it is still in effect. [2]

THE ALASKA ZOO in Anchorage was founded in 1967 by Sammye Seawell, who built it around Annabelle, an Asian elephant that a friend of hers won in a contest. Annabelle was a star attraction for thirty years, but she became more than just a passive tenant. Annabelle painted with her trunk. Her work drew gulps from art critics but raves from families visiting the zoo. Hundreds of Annabelle's paintings were sold through the zoo's gift shop, raising thousands of dollars to help support her fellow animals.

YOU NEVER QUITE KNEW what to expect from Geoff Kennedy when he went on the air. While working at a Fairbanks radio station, he offered a heartfelt obituary for a cat. Here's part of it:

A voice was stilled in the Stevenson household Monday night. Not just any voice. In fact, the voice may have set the all-time Fairbanks North Star Borough record for meowing, both for longevity and frequency.

Unlike other felines, Ranger did not save her meows for special occasions like "Feed me," "Let me out," or "Change my litterbox." Ranger's meows meant, as far as I can tell, "I'm here, and don't you forget it." And she kept that up for nineteen years.

Now, Ranger's articulation did not stop at just meowing. If you accidentally sat on Her Majesty's throne, Ranger would display her repertoire of hissing and growling. But meowing remained her specialty. Particularly the generic meow. She'd walk into a room, look around, and start complaining something did not meet her expectations. Which was most of the time.

Ranger had an attitude. What Hall of Fame Green Bay Packer Jerry Kramer once said of his coach, Vince Lombardi, could be said of Ranger, too: "Underneath that gruff exterior lies a gruff interior."

GOVERNOR WALTER HICKEL created a fury when he authorized game biologists to shoot wolves from the air as a way to protect caribou from hungry wolves. A group of environmentalists in the Seattle area started encouraging tourists to boycott Alaska until the shooting stopped.

One young counter-protester showed up at the Alaska State Ferry terminal in Bellingham, Washington, carrying a poster depicting a masked man holding a pistol in a wolf's mouth. His sign read: "Visit Alaska This Summer or the Wolf Bites It!"

YOUNG BALD EAGLES have an understandable tendency to defer to larger birds. When a young eagle is flying off with prey and finds itself challenged by a larger eagle, the smaller bird will often drop its catch and flee, hoping to avoid a fight.

That tendency caused a problem for an airliner in 1987. A young eagle was flying high over Juneau, carrying a freshly caught salmon in its talons, when an Alaska Airlines 737 took off from Juneau Airport. The eagle saw the 737 below, must have decided the jetliner was a really, really big bird, and dropped the fish. The eagle got away clean, but the salmon splintered the plane's windshield, requiring a damage inspection stop at Yakutat.

THE WALRUS IS BLESSED with an ivory penis bone which, when removed from the animal, often becomes a gift certain to make its recipient blush. The unique nature of this bone—the oosik—inspired this well-known ribald poem.

Strange things have been done in the Midnight Sun,
and the storybooks are full;
But the strangest tale concerns the male,
magnificent walrus bull.

I know it's rude, quite common and crude,
perhaps it is grossly unkind;
But with first glance at least, this bewhiskered beast,
is as ugly in front as behind.

How can this be, this clandestine glee
that exudes from the walrus like music?
He knows there inside, beneath blubber and hide
lies a splendid contrivance—the Oosik!

"Oosik" you say—and quite well you may,
I'll explain if you keep it between us;
In the simplest truth, though rather uncouth,
"Oosik" is, in fact, his penis!
Now the size alone of this walrus bone
would indeed arouse envious thinking;
It is also a fact, documented and backed,
there is never a softening or shrinking.

This, then, is why the smile is so sly,
the walrus is rightfully proud.
Though the climate is frigid, the walrus is rigid;
Pray, why is not man so endowed?

Added to this is a smile you might miss—
though the bull is entitled to bow—
The one to out-smile our bull by a mile
is the satisfied walrus cow!

Tourists say the darnedest things. One wanted to go on a sled dog ride—the same way you ride a horse.

4 | Tourists
What Time Is the One O'clock Tour?

After thirty years of herding reindeer, Chester Seveck retired and became a tour guide in Fairbanks. "Same job," he liked to say. [1]

ALASKA TOURISTS SAY the darnedest things, to judge by these comments collected by the Anchorage Convention and Visitors Bureau:

"Where can we change our money into Alaska money?"

"Where is the Empire State Building?"

"What time of year can you drive your car across the Bering Strait?"

"What time does your one o'clock tour start?"

"Where can I photograph penguins?" (The correct answer: In the Antarctic, about 9,000 miles south of Anchorage.)

One man wanted to go on a sled dog ride. He thought you ride a sled dog the way you ride a horse.

A woman called from Chicago to ask if Alaska has grocery stores or if she should bring her own food.

A man called from Sacramento to ask: "Does it always snow between 9 a.m. and 4 p.m.?"

A woman from Tennessee asked: "Where can I go to meet Alaska men?" (It's tempting to suggest that she heed the words of the sage who said: "Alaska has more men than women. But beware, the odds are good but the goods are odd.")

NORTH SLOPE OIL WORKERS see their share of tourists. Melissa Pesanti was hosting a group at the ARCO visitors center when one greenhorn asked: "When does a caribou turn into a moose?"

Melissa didn't even blink. "September." she said, "We call them cariboose. Any other questions?" [2]

IT WAS A CLASH of cultures the day the straight-laced parents of Sophia Anna List first discovered moose droppings and oosiks.

The Lists were in Alaska to visit their daughter and to see the state for the first time. Shopping with Sophia, they soon bought some postcards and some ulus (Eskimo women's knives).

Writer Mary Barry tells what happens when they came across an oosik, the justly famous penis bone of the walrus: [3]

Papa List spotted a long, gray object made of bone in the midst of some ivory carvings.

"What is the purpose of this?" he asked. "Except for the ivory carvings on the ends, it doesn't look particularly artistic to me."

"That is an oosik, Pa," said Sophia, turning a pale pink.

"An oosik? What is its significance? What is it made of?"

"It's—well, it comes from a walrus—"

"Oh, a walrus tusk! I thought they were whiter and thicker."

"No, it's not exactly from that end—you know, walruses are awfully obese and flabby, so when they—"

At that moment, to Sophia's relief, her mother called out, wanting to know the origin of those brownish, rounded oval objects attached to swizzle sticks, ear drops, and necklaces.

"Those are moose nuggets, Ma," explained Sophia.

"Moose nuggets? I've heard of gold nuggets and copper nuggets, but how do they get nuggets from moose? Are they some sort of mineral deposit, like gallstones?"

"No, not really. In fact, the moose nuggets are obtained from the moose with absolutely no harm to the animal."

"Tell me the background of them!"

"Well, the moose nugget artisans go out into parts of the forest frequented by moose. If they are lucky, they will find piles of moose droppings in good condition—well-shaped, dry and separated—which they take to their workshops, cover with plastic, and fashion into novelty items for tourists."

"Do you mean," said Sophia's mother, with a disgusted look on her face, "I've been handling moose doo-doo?"

"That's it, Ma! That's basically what a moose nugget is."

KENAI RIVER FISHING GUIDE Gary Galbraith once had eight middle-aged men and women from Japan with him. Not one spoke a word of English.

"The leader of the group hooked into a big Dolly Varden," Galbraith says. "It was maybe twenty-four inches long, weighing about five pounds. We're getting it up to the boat, getting it up. I had the net ready. I was just ready to scoop it out of the water, and they're all standing up in the boat clapping.

"But then the guy who had the fish on his line started clapping too."

The rod fell over the side and into the water.

"They all just sat down and didn't say a word." [4]

BACKCOUNTRY HIKERS are often urged to wear little bells on their clothing when traveling in bear country. The bells help to scare away black bears and most grizzlies—but not necessarily the coastal brown bears, the largest and meanest of the lot.

When visitors ask how to tell which kind of bears are around, they are told to watch for droppings.

"How do you tell which is which?" the visitors inevitably ask.

"The brown-bear poop is full of little bells," answer the locals.

SEVENTEEN-YEAR-OLD Kris Jensen was camping at Byers Lake with three of his buddies and noticed two couples setting up a tent nearby. One couple was from Texas, the other from California. Kris and his friends said hello to the visitors and warned them about bears.

Don't worry, the couples assured them; they already knew they had to put their food where bears couldn't get to it. Then both parties headed off in different directions to fish and hike.

When Kris and his buddies returned, they found the neighboring campsite torn to shreds. The tent was slashed. Bedding, clothes, and food containers were scattered through the woods. Around the camp were the tracks of a black bear sow and two cubs.

The tourists were mystified about the damage. They said they had heeded the warning about bears and hid their food under the tent.

MOST OF ALASKA'S VISITORS go home and tell their friends about the trip. A few visitors have even larger audiences. Dave Barry's syndicated humor column reaches millions, and here's what he had to say about Alaska:

My family and I recently returned from a trip to Alaska, a place that combines spectacular natural beauty with a breathtaking amount of tax deductibility if you write a travel article about it, which is what I'm doing here. I'll start with some Facts at a Glance:

Where Alaska is: Way the hell far from you. Beyond Mars.

How you get there: You sit in a variety of airplanes for the bulk of your adult life (longer if you take a child.)

What they have there that will try to kill you: Bears. I am quite serious about this. Although Alaska is now an official United State with modern conveniences such as rental cars and frozen yogurt, it also contains a large number of admitted bears, striding freely about the landscape, and nobody seems to be the least bit alarmed about this. In fact, the Alaskans seem to be proud of it. You walk into a hotel or department store, and the first thing you see is a glass case containing a stuffed bear the size of Nigeria. Our hotel had two of these. It was what we travel writers call "a two-bear hotel." Both bears were standing on their hind legs and striking a pose that said: "Welcome to Alaska! I'm going to rip your arms off."

This struck me as an odd concept, greeting visitors with a showcase containing a major local hazard. It's as if the Greater Miami Chamber of Commerce went around setting up glass display cases containing stuffed cocaine smugglers, with little plaques stating how much they weighed and where they were taken. (Which is not such a bad idea, now that I think of it.)

Anyway, we decided the best way to deal with our fear of bears was to become well-informed about them, so we bought a book titled "Alaska Bear Tales." Here are some of the chapter titles, which I am not making up:

"They'll Attack Without Warning"

"They'll Really Maul You"

"They Will Kill"

"Come Quick! I'm Being Eaten by a Bear!"

"They Can Be Funny"

Ha ha! I bet they can. I bet Mr. and Mrs. Bear are a bundle of hilarity as they tussle playfully over the remaining portion of a former tourist plumped up by airline food. But just the same, I'm glad that the only actual, non-stuffed practicing bears that we saw were in the Anchorage Zoo.

We did, however, see a great deal of nature. Alaska is almost completely covered with nature, including several million spectacular snow-capped mountains, any one of which is so awesome that if you were to relocate it to an average semiflat state such as Indiana, the residents would all quit their jobs and form cults and worship it.

But Alaska has so many amazing mountains that after a while you hardly notice them, which is a good thing because it frees you to watch out for the moose poop, which is all over the place in the form of egg-shaped units known as "moose nuggets," which local people use—this is also the truth—to make earrings and other souvenir items to sell to tourists who have no taste or decency. We bought some.

Speaking of the local people, they are as nice as any we've ever met. This is probably because there are only about eighty-five of them, and they all seem to know each other. It's an informal state, the kind of state where if you stayed for a couple of weeks and didn't shoot anybody, they'd probably let you be lieutenant governor. (Alaska has a fully operational state government, complete with buildings, legislature, etc. The front-page issue being hotly debated while we were there was: salmon.)

As you'd expect, Alaskans tend to be hardy, outdoor-oriented individuals. For most of us, a real Wilderness Adventure is to operate a non-riding lawn mower.

A rugged Alaskan we met was Cynthia Toohey, who operates the Crow Creek Mine near Anchorage. This is a genuine gold mine, with a sign on the entrance road stating:

No Shooting

No Fern Picking!

Toohey lives in a house with no electricity, phone or plumbing, and no way to get in or out during winter except by snowmobile. "When the tourists come," she said, "they ask me, 'How can you get by without a trash compactor?'" She had Pepsi cooling in a snowbank and a loaded gun over the front door. I asked her if she'd ever had any trouble with bears, and she said, yeah, she had; but she seemed more concerned about fern-pickers.

Not far from the Crow Creek Mine is the Bird House, *is now located 3 doors West of us.* a tiny truly wonderful bar that is falling down a hillside and has reached such a steep angle that if you don't hang on to your beer bottle, it will slide away and fall off the bar. Not that this would matter: You couldn't possibly make a mess in the Bird House, because it already contains two-thirds of the world clutter supply. Every surface is covered with objects left by patrons—business cards, underpants, numerous brassieres (some the size of tank parachutes) and, of course, an artificial leg.

Alaska also contains glaciers, avalanches, earthquakes and a large quantity of "tundra" (an Eskimo word meaning "nothing"). These are all very important in terms of geology, and you should definitely visit them. But stop by the Bird House first. And save your receipts.

In Alaska, mosquitoes are large flying predators that come in two sizes, twin-engined and four-engined.

5 | Word Play
Alaskan Spoken Here

An Anchorage health official offered this astute obser-vation on the dangers of carbon monoxide poisoning: "By the time you have symptoms, you've been exposed."

ALASKANS HAVE A special language, with words and meanings all their own. Here is a brief glossary, cour-tesy of Anchorage newspaper columnist Mike Doogan: [1]

Alaskan. Anyone who had a chance to leave but didn't.

Alaskans. The smartest, toughest, funniest, best-look-ing, friendliest people in the whole world. Just ask one.

Cheechako (chee-CHA-koh). A newcomer to Alaska, usually one who has not survived a winter here. The word comes from Chinook jargon, a combination of English and Indian dialects once used by traders. As any sourdough will tell you, cheechakos are an inferior breed that don't know nuthin'.

Cold. According to physicists, there is no such thing as cold, only an absence of heat. Alaska is missing a hell of a lot of heat during the winter. The greatest absence of heat ever recorded in Alaska was minus eighty at Prospect Creek Camp on January 23, 1971.

Dog musher. The driver of a dog team who, when not serving as the dogs' cook and valet, spends a lot of time looking at their south ends.

Freeze-up. What an Alaskan's brain does when the ground gets hard enough to bend a pick-axe and the dog's water dish ices over. Freeze-up is caused by the realization that another winter has come much too soon and will stay much too long.

Greenie. One of the less derogatory terms for an environmentalist. Greenies believe that no road in Alaska is so useful that the state wouldn't be better off without it.

Hoochino. What the old-timers always drank and modern Alaskans sometimes drink too. Hooch, for short, was alcohol made from whatever was handy, left to ferment for the shortest possible time.

Mosquito. In Alaska, this is not a bug at all, but a large flying predator. Alaska mosquitoes come in two sizes, twin-engined and four-engined, but only one temperament—mean. The smaller variety are a threat to household pets and small children, the larger kind a menace to livestock and small cars.

Outside. Every place under the American flag but Alaska. Outside is a bad, bad place that's home to evil bureaucrats, rabid greenies, and corrupt politicians, all bent on keeping Alaskans from earning an honest fortune. It's also the place most Alaskans came from.

Sourdough. This word originally meant a yeasty concoction with a long life, used to leaven bread and pancakes in the early days. Now it's often applied to anyone who looks ancient enough to have used the stuff. It's said that sourdoughs stay on in Alaska because, even though they are sour on the land, they don't have the dough to leave.

Sourdough hotcakes. Long a miner's staple, these delicacies should be tough on the outside and tender on the inside. If not eaten right out of the pan, they are best used to shingle the roof.

Summer. A brief period of bright sun and warm air, usually on a Thursday afternoon in July or August.

ALASKANS HAVE A WAY with words, even if it's by mistake. Tom Jensen was working in television news at Anchorage's KTVA Channel 11 when he reported a story about a bear mauling. But his tongue slipped.

The story as reported by Jensen: "A 39-year-old man was balled by a bear today."

ALASKA RADIO PESONALITY Geoff Kennedy remembers one listener who called in to counter the perception that gay men are necessarily effeminate. "Essentially," the caller said, "you can't tell a homosexual from any Joe Blow."

CONGRESSMAN DON YOUNG has had his moments of battle with the English language. "You may not agree with everything I say," he once stated, "but you have to admit I'm a man of quantity."

Young is known in Washington, D.C., as the man who gave a congressional colleague the finger on the floor of the House and who brought a walrus penis bone (an *oosik*) into the sometimes somber legislative chamber.

He once made ribald comments to a Fairbanks high school audience and later explained during a grilling by the editorial board of the *Anchorage Daily News*: "I'm not a politician, I've never been a politician. I mean, if I was a politician, do you think I'd say some of the things I've said?"

During a radio interview the Congressman applauded an effort to strengthen the work of the commission charged with oversight of salmon in North Pacific waters. Young said he was encouraged that the commission would be "reinvigorished and reburgerated."

Congressman Young's assaults on the language sometimes seem to improve on it. He once dismissed an opponent's arguments as "bladderdash."

THEN THERE WAS THE TIME Alaska Senator Ted Stevens stood on the floor of the Senate and said: "Before I make the statement that I intend to make, though, I would like to ask my friend a question, and before I ask that question, I'll make a statement of my own." That one made the *New York Times*.

A STATE LEGISLATOR once made the startling observation: "I think the 1990s is going to be a new decade."

WALTER J. HICKEL has never feared to speak his mind, but his tongue has occasionally outraced his imposing intellect. While serving a second term as Alaska's governor, Hickel once said a proposed constitutional amendment was a bad idea because "it does not meet the needs of rural residents who live in urban areas."

And then there was: "You have to look where you came

from to know where you're going. If you don't know where you're going and you haven't been anyplace, there's a risk."

One day in 1970, while Hickel was serving as Secretary of the Interior, he received an angry letter from Senator Joseph Montoya of New Mexico. Hickel was outraged. Hickel's assistant Dave Parker urged him to dictate a response. "Take down this telegram," Hickel shouted. "Fuck you! Strong letter follows." Cooler heads prevailed and the telegram was never sent. [2]

Hickel is also remembered for uttering the classic line: "You can't just let nature run wild."

EVEN JUNIOR ALASKANS know how to use the English language to surprise their listeners. Larry Holmstrom was once doing a live television interview with a young boy whose goat had just won a second-place ribbon in the Fairbanks 4-H competition. And why didn't the goat take top honors, Holmstrom asked.

"Because he shit on the judge," the boy answered.

ONE AFTERNOON WHEN he was about four years old, my son Tobin wandered into the basement where I was puttering.

"Hi Toby," I said. "Where's Mom?"

A look of wonder crossed his face and he answered: "She's upstairs, layin' on the bed with nothin' on."

"Oh?" I asked, various thoughts running through my mind.

"Yeah," he said. "No lights, no radio, no television . . . nothin'."

A man walked out of a downtown Anchorage bar, saw a bear on the sidewalk and swore off drinking on the spot.

6 | Bear with Me
There's Trouble A'bruin

Mike Doogan says the best bear protection is to go hiking with companions who run slower than you do. [1]

BEARS IN LOVE . . . bears at the McDonald's restaurant . . . bears up a creek . . . bears in the country and bears in the city. These are stories about bears — and they're all true.

DURING CONSTRUCTION of the trans-Alaska pipeline, wildlife agent Tom Buhite received a call from a worried medical technician at Five-Mile Camp. The man thought a grizzly might be hibernating under the temporary building housing his medical facility.

"What makes you think so?" Buhite asked.

"I can hear him snoring."

Buhite drove to the camp and shined a flashlight under the building. He couldn't see anything, so he and the medic crawled around on the floor, listening with a stethoscope. Next day he called his boss, Ben Hilliker.

"There's definitely a bear under there," Buhite said. "What do you want me to do?"

"Leave him alone," Hilliker said. "He'll go away in the spring."

JAY HAMMOND ONCE worked as a government wolf trapper, spending much of his time in the wilderness. He often encountered bears but rarely had trouble with them—until one day on Big River. The governor-to-be found himself in close quarters with a bear that had been chasing a moose, then turned its attentions to Hammond. The bear charged, and Hammond had to shoot.

Hammond was embarrassed by the incident; he had been proud of his ability to deal with the huge animals without shooting them. He dutifully filed a report with the U.S. Fish and Wildlife Service office, a report soon uncovered by a newspaper reporter. The writer's imagination was fired, especially by details manufactured and passed on by Hammond's mischievous fellow agent, Bob Burkholder.

Here's what the reporter had to say in his article:

Hammond, a rather large fellow, commonly wears one of those hairy Canadian sweaters. A wolf trapper by trade, not surprisingly he often smells something other than human. Given how brown bear have very poor eyesight and this was the mating season, you get the picture. To put it delicately, to save himself from a "fate worse than death," according to Burkholder, "Hammond had no choice but to shoot the amorous animal whose only crime was to fall in love."[2]

SEVERAL YOUNG BROWN BEARS showed up in rather crowded areas of Anchorage during the fall of 1999. One woman stopped at a McDonald's drive-through window, picked up her order, then started to leave. At the end of the driveway she encountered a brown bear, threw her car into reverse, and roared back past the drive-through window. Later that same night a man walked out of a downtown saloon, saw a brown bear on the sidewalk and swore off drinking on the spot.

THE BEAR CAME OUT the winner in this story told by author Kathy Hunter:

Mac was an Irish immigrant, a bachelor who may have been the first to homestead the south bank of the Kenai River. He chose to live on an old bear trail, and so was occasionally bothered by curious or hungry bears. He lost patience with them one time, and the results were nearly disastrous.

Mac had been bothered by one bear in particular, a bear that came in the dark and caused havoc around his place looking for food. One night, taking courage from home brew, Mac tied some meat on a rope. He placed it on the ground outside the cabin, brought the rope through the window, and tied the other end around his ankle. Then, he waited in bed with a loaded gun.

During the night the bear came and grabbed the meat. Mac was asleep, and woke up yelling. Scared by the noise, the bear took off with the meat, dragging the hollering man halfway through the window. At that point the rope came untied to release Mac, who sobered up in a hurry. [3]

SGT. JOHN WALDREN, a village protection safety officer in Yakutat, received a call about a man who had climbed a tree near the Situk River and refused to come down.

Waldren went to the river and found a German fisherman who had been walking the riverbank with a trophy steelhead trout on his stringer when a large brown bear approached. The man dropped the fish and scampered up the tree. The bear ate the fish, then walked to the tree and began batting at its trunk, trying to shake the fisherman loose. The man clung terrified to his perch, refusing to come down even after the bear wandered into the brush and other fishermen happened by.

The officer tried to coax the man down, but he adamantly refused. "OK," Waldren said, "we'll have to leave you there and head back to town. But you should know that bears can climb trees."

A stricken look crossed the man's face as he shouted,: "Wait for me!" [4]

ONE DAY DURING World War II, some soldiers in Alaska were part of a welcome instance of peaceful coexistence. A black bear woke from hibernation and wandered into an open-air service being conducted at an Army post in the Territory. The chaplain continued his preaching and the soldiers continued praying; the bear stretched out in the sun and listened. When the services ended, the bear stretched, yawned, and wandered away. [5]

BOB BELL WAS FISHING for red salmon on Wolverine Creek, north of Anchorage. He had brought a rifle, since Wolverine Creek is in prime brown bear country, and leaned the gun against a tree while he waded in to fish.

After a while, a group of fishermen across the creek shouted to Bob. He turned to see what was up—and saw that a bear had grabbed his rifle. The bear had the rifle in its mouth, like a dog with a stick.

Bob asked the other fishermen to back him up with their rifle while he dealt with the bear. Standing thigh-deep in water, Bell grabbed a large rock and tossed it at the brownie. The missile hit the animal square between the ears. It dropped the rifle, ran about a hundred feet, then stood woofing and snapping its jaws. Bob tiptoed over to the rifle, picked it up, and walked—hurriedly—back to his airplane.

MILITARY POLICE at the Ballistic Missile Early Warning System at Clear received a call from the base commander's office—but they heard only the sounds of heavy breathing and noises of an apparent struggle taking place. The policemen rushed to the office and met a bear coming out. The animal had broken into the office and somehow hit the phone and opened the line while rooting around on the desk. [6]

CHARLIE EVANS, one of the dog mushers who relayed diphtheria serum to Nome in 1923, told about his two sons leaving their boat to go hunting in the brush. When they returned, they found a black bear rummaging through their gear. But this bear had unusual tastes. It threw aside groceries, coffee, tea, and sugar until it found what it was after: two packs of cigarettes. The bear wandered off with the smokes in its mouth. Was this the original Smoky the Bear? [7]

AN ALASKAN HOUSEHOLD HINT, contributed by Miki and Julie Collins: "A painless way to eliminate hornet nests is to have a small bear around. A nice little bear that only comes out at night, who will dig up nests to eat the larvae. One bear destroyed dozens of nests on our hill, some within a few yards of our home. Of course, you want a black bear, not a grizzly. Grizzlies are even more scary than hornets." [8]

Cecilia Braund used to say if her age ever caught up with her bust size, she was going to throw one hell of a party.

7 | People of the North Country

You'll Never Call 'Em Ordinary

It takes a special person to live in Alaska—some would say a person who doesn't have both oars in the water. A friend in Anchorage claims that North America is like a hot fudge sundae, with all the nuts on top.

YOU'RE AN ALASKAN if you:
- design your Halloween costume to fit over a snowsuit.   *Done that!*
- have more miles on your snow blower than your car.
- have ten favorite recipes for halibut.
- believe driving is better in the winter because the potholes are filled with snow.
- think sexy lingerie is tube socks and a flannel nightie with only eight buttons.
- owe more money on your snowmachine than your car.
- believe the start of caribou or moose season should be a national holiday.
- know that summer takes place the second week of July.

- feel that a temperature of minus twenty degrees is a little chilly.
- use the trunk of your car to double as a deep freezer.
- know the four seasons: Almost Winter, Winter, Still Winter, and Construction. [1]

WRITER KATHY HUNTER tells of Cantwell Alice of Talkeetna:

Alice was a woman gandy dancer. They said that the portion of railroad track she hammered was the smoothest of all, and that she could outswing and outcurse any man. She was also a better poker player.

Once, someone asked Alice if she knew the candidate for mayor. "I ought to," she said. "I have three of his kids."

BARROW ENTREPRENEUR Fran Tate decided that the tank truck owned by the government-owned honey bucket service was too small and inefficient—and that the town's streets were taking on an unpleasant odor as a result. She founded a competing service, called the Elephant Pot Sewage Hauling Company. Its motto: "We clean up your act because we've got our shit together."

Tate later opened a Mexican food restaurant in Barrow, Pepe's North of the Border, which became known as the world's northernmost Mexican food joint. Less well understood was the fact that—with the Elephant Pot Sewage Hauling Company—Fran's enterprises were the northernmost vertically integrated business, handling food products from manufacture through service and consumption to disposal of the end product.

Tate, a blond-haired engineer who moved to Barrow in

1970, was married six times. Writer Lyn Kidder quotes Fran describing her split-up with her second husband:

> One night I fixed fish for dinner, and he didn't come home at five, six, seven, eight. . . . About ten o'clock I just put all his clothes and belongings out on the front porch with his dinner—a plate with fish on it and a potato. And a note: "Don't bother to come in." Of course about midnight he came pounding on the door, but I just said, "That's it! I'm done! No more!"

> And he was yelling, "I can't live without you, I'm going to shoot myself!" Then I remembered, I forgot to put out his gun, so I got it and threw it out the door, too. [2]

"RED EYE WAS A rather loud truck driver who fancied a waitress named Sheila in a cafe in Glennallen," writes Kathy Hunter.

> One day, when Sheila was dead tired, Red Eye came in and ordered a bowl of soup. As Sheila brought the soup to the counter, she tripped and fell forward. Sheila didn't spill a drop, but her left thumb slipped into the bowl.

> Sheila had her thumb halfway to her mouth when Red Eye caught it in midair. "I'll be paying for a full bowl of soup and I want it all!" he said, and thrust her soupy thumb into his own mouth. Sheila immediately doubled her right fist, and let him have it on the jaw. Red Eye crashed backward to the floor, landing on his head.

> Sheila eyed her fist in wonder. The other truckers looked at Red Eye on the floor, then went back to eating. Eventually, the bull cook revived Red Eye with a bucket of cold water.

> "Your soup's getting cold, mister," Sheila announced.

A week later, Red Eye arrived at the cafe with a dozen roses and a new attitude. Sheila served him soup, without thumb. Six trips later, during dinner, he proposed over the soup course. Sheila thought it over while he ate the special of the day, then delivered a positive answer with dessert. [3]

AUTHOR BETH DAY gives an illuminating glimpse into the style of pilot Archie Ferguson:

Madman Archie Ferguson decided there never had been anything as much fun as a plane radio to fool with and kept up a running monologue during all his flights, describing his every motion in a high-pitched screech that drowned out all other transmissions.

When he also developed the endearing trick of carrying on family feuds with his wife, who had a transmitter at their trading post, CAA personnel ordered him off the air "unless there is an emergency."

"Hell," screeched Archie, "any time I'm flyin' it's an emergency!"

BOB ATWOOD of *The Anchorage Times* once assigned reporter Margaret Schmidt to call Municipal Light & Power to ask if the utility could turn the clocks of Anchorage an hour ahead in spring by sending an extra surge of power through the system.

The utility manager politely explained that such a surge would blow out a lot of electrical transformers but would not advance the clocks.

"We could turn them back in the fall by turning the power off for an hour," he added. "Of course, that would shut the city down."

When told of the utility's response, Atwood said: "You never know until you ask."

THE REVEREND RICHARD TERO was conducting a renewal retreat for parishioners of Saint Patrick's Church in Anchorage's Muldoon neighborhood. One of his main points: Catholics should be more mindful of their identities as Catholics and more careful about the constant distractions of the secular culture around them.

The retreat on the last weekend of October 1986 coincided with the World Series. And Father Tero was a lifelong fan of the Red Sox, who were going head to head with the New York Mets.

At one point in the retreat, the parishioners were waiting for their pastor's scheduled appearance. They waited . . . and waited . . . and waited—but no Father Tero.

You guessed it: Father Tero apparently sat mesmerized before a TV set until the bitter (for the Red Sox) end of that day's ball game.

He suddenly remembered his congregation and went scrambling back to the church, where he was puzzled to find the lights turned out. When he flicked the switch, the congregation broke out singing, "Take me out to the ball game."

A red-faced Father Tero quickly recovered, even using himself as proof of his message: "See what I mean about secular influences on our Catholicism?" [4]

WHEN KFAR WENT on the air in 1939, Fairbanks got its first radio station, and broadcasting pioneer Augie Hiebert and his small team of professionals became a major source of information of all kinds. Robin Ann Chlupach,

Augie's daughter, wrote about one of KFAR's on-air personalities and the ingenuity the Hiebert team used to entertain their audiences:

Bud Foster was a master at sporting event re-creations. Many local sporting events were broadcast live, but not major league baseball or even the World Series. Fairbanks loved baseball, and they were dependent on Bud to bring baseball to them "live."

There were three keys to Bud's re-creations: his props, a relay system of information, and Bud himself. A pencil striking a small piece of wood simulated the crack of the bat. A pencil striking a roll of toilet paper was the sound of the ball hitting the catcher's mitt. Crowd noise came from a recorded disc.

The relay arrangement worked via Alaska Communications System (ACS). Twenty-five words or so an inning would come over the telegraph, and a runner would pick up the message from ACS each inning and deliver it to Bud. Bud knew the game of baseball, and from bits and pieces he would masterfully reproduce an entire ballgame. With his vivid portrayals you were there!

Once in the middle of a game, the wire went out and no more reports came through. Bud stalled—a rain delay here, a news report there, then another rain delay. Finally the game resumed. The wire service may have failed, but Bud did not. No one ever knew if Bud's final score approximated the real one, but he kept the game going! [5]

HUMORIST GARRISON KEILLOR had great fun with the Alaska mystique when he sang this song during a broadcast of *A Prairie Home Companion* from Anchorage in 1996. It's to the tune of "California Girls" and is dedicated to Kirsten Dixon and her staff at Finger Lake Lodge. [6]

Well, Homer Girls are hip, I really dig that herbal tea.
And the Fairbanks Girls collect oil drums, spend the winter in their RVs.
The Barrow Girls live in the dark, so they always mystify.
And the Juneau Girls are forever young cuz their skin does not get dry.
I wish they all could be Matanuska Girls.

Well, Matanuska Girls can run a snowmachine all day,
but they also know a French Bordeaux from a domestic cabernet.
They hunt for moose and bear and bring them back in from the wild
And skin the furs and fix a perfect dish by Julia Child.
I wish they all could be Matanuska Girls.

Well, Matanuska Girls they bring in salmon, ducks, and geese.
They're also smart about great art like Picasso and Matisse.
They can use an ax or welding torch with maximum finesse
And then look great on a dinner date in a black Armani dress.
I wish they all could be Matanuska Girls.

They're crazy and they're subtle and they're funny and profound.
They've got their dreams and yet it seems, they've got their boots on solid ground.

They do quite well in darkness and in steady rain or snow
And they do real fine in warm sunshine, they can make
*   your garden grow.*
I wish they all could be Matanuska Girls.

ALASKA IS KNOWN for its prominent features, including the voluminous breasts of Cecilia "Ceil" Braund. Ceil was known widely for her raucous and intensely naughty sense of humor. Hers is a funny, bittersweet story and her obituary, reprinted in part here with permission of the *Anchorage Daily News*, is an Alaska classic. It appeared March 20, 1987.

So Long, Cecilia
By Debbie McKinney

She preyed on flat-chested women: "Wanna hear a joke that will make your boobs fall off? Oh, I see you've already heard it."

And she was quick to divulge the facts: "Get the vital statistics down straight. My measurements from the bottom up are 37-29-49 1/2 with a bra on. Without a bra on, I'm 37-46-32. On my hands and knees, I'm 37-29-63."

Cecilia "Ceil" Braund used to say if her age ever caught up with her bust size, she's going to throw "one hell of a party." She didn't make it. Ceil died Monday morning of kidney failure. She was 46.

Ceil was an institution in the watering holes around Indian, most recently as manager of the now-defunct Bore Tide bar. The few who knew the woman behind the antics saw a sensitive, warmhearted person who valued her time alone, devoured books and expressed herself best through poetry. The countless many who didn't saw only the flamboyant wigs, furlined miniskirts and mammoth-sized mammaries. But then, you'd have to be blind not to see them. They weighed more than 14 pounds apiece and were insured by Lloyd's of London.

Ceil's clothes were custom made to flaunt what she considered her best attribute. Consequently, she always looked on the verge of falling out of her dress. But that only happened when she wanted it to.

Particularly during the pipeline days, men would line up to be photographed grinning with their heads buried amid Ceil's appendages, one on each side. "Alaska earmuffs," she called them.

Ceil especially liked the little old men from Florida who wanted Alaska earmuff pictures to hang in their retirement homes. She'd give them their earmuffs and they'd hobble off as happy as could be. That's what Ceil decided these anomalies were for: to make others happy.

Ceil was married five times. Her first marriage to a sailor lasted about 20 hours. "I was 14 and he was 28," she once said. "After we got married, we went to a motel room and he called his mother long distance and asked her what to do. So I packed my bags and had it annulled."

Ceil had started writing a book before she died. A description of the bicycle trip was the last thing she wrote: "We had four water jugs, one with VO and one with vodka and two with water. Let me tell you, you cannot drink and ride. It zaps all your strength. Plus, it seems your bike doesn't want to go straight. Neither did my (breasts). And wherever (they) go, I go and my bike and half the traffic."

Near panic struck before a businessman confessed he'd hired a helicopter to throw burning tires into the volcano.

8 | Impractical Jokes
It's Funny When It Happens to the Other Guy

It was April 1. Clint Andrews at the Anchorage Daily News *reported that the Anchorage Telephone Utility would clean its lines that day and advised homeowners to put a pillowcase or blanket over their phones to keep dust from blowing into their homes. Some did.*

ALASKA'S MOST FAMOUS April Fool's Day joke occurred in 1974 when the people of Sitka awoke to see black smoke belching from the mouth of Mount Edgecumbe, the massive volcano just across Sitka Sound from the city.

Sitka's tsunami siren was sounded and near panic developed about the volcano's impending eruption. Finally, businessman Porky Bickar admitted he had hired a helicopter and ferried a pile of rubber tires into the volcano's cone, then set them afire.

Anchorage radio personality Geoff Kennedy is known for his April Fool's Day newscasts. Such as:

The State House has passed a bill to rename the

Ten Commandments. The bill's sponsor, Jim Mitchell of Sterling, wants them called the Ten Opportunities. Kennedy quoted Mitchell as saying: "I'm simply asking for a moral code that is more user-friendly."

President Clinton and House Speaker Newt Gingrich don't agree on much, but both are disputing the results of a new medical study that suggests pot smoking causes men to dodge the draft, turn into politicians, chase women, and break campaign finance laws.

The State Legislature is suing a Kodiak man for defamation of character. Jerry Sandusky labeled legislators "a bunch of bozos" for passing a tort reform law last year. To make matters worse, the Bunch of Bozos Anti-Defamation League has sued Sandusky for comparing them to legislators.

LIKE MANY NEWS PEOPLE, Tom Jensen eventually went into public relations, working for RCA Alascom. One day he received a call from a radio reporter who wanted to ask about the semiannual problem in which satellite broadcast coverage is lost briefly due to the satellite's alignment with the sun.

"Can you fix it?" the reporter asked.

Jensen put his tongue firmly in his cheek and answered. "Oh yeah. We're working on changing the orbit of the sun."

In her broadcast that night, the reporter took Jensen at his word. She told a statewide audience that RCA Alascom was planning to change the orbit of the sun.

WHEN ALBRO GREGORY was editor of the *Nome Nugget*, the city fathers replaced the historic Front Street boardwalk with a paved sidewalk. Front Street was Nome's main thoroughfare and ran in front of the *Nugget* office. Gregory, a colorful man and Ernest Hemingway look-alike, printed an angry editorial denouncing "the evils of progress."

The next day, someone installed a parking meter in front of the office—the only parking meter in the entire town.

MY WIFE AND I were on a train running between Anchorage and Fairbanks and listening intently to the conductor's running spiel. As the car rumbled onto the trestle over Hurricane Canyon, the conductor said, "Down on the right side of the train, at the bottom of the canyon, you can just see the wreckage of an old train."

Along with all the other passengers, we ran to the right side of the car and pressed our faces to the window, peering intently down into the canyon. We couldn't spot the wrecked train but assumed it must be too close to the trestle for us to see.

One of the passengers asked, "How did it get there?"

The conductor laughed and said, "It happened one day when all the passengers ran to one side of the train and it tipped over."

WRANGELL THEATER MANAGER Dick Ballard was on the receiving end of a practical joke dreamed up by Dick Stough, who was known for such tricks, and Dick's wife, Yvonne, along with Des Moore and Howard Brand of Ketchikan.

They printed flyers that said "Kiddies, Have a Free Show and a Treat on Uncle Dick," telling readers to hurry on over to Ballard's theater. The conspirators enlisted Earl Lahmeyer to airdrop the flyers over Wrangell. The papers drifted down over the town, and soon kids were showing up at the theater to claim their free show and treat. [1]

NOW IT CAN BE TOLD, since the evidence melted long ago.

One winter evening during the reign of Governor Jay Hammond, two executives of the state Division of Oil and Gas were sympathizing with each other about all the industry regulations and study reports being demanded of them by their boss, Natural Resources Commissioner Bob LeResche. Division director Tom Cook and petroleum engineer John Miller spent several hours that evening in a Juneau tavern, fuming about the situation.

As they left the bar, they spotted LeResche across the street, deep in a discussion with another official.

"There's that rascal now," Cook muttered.

Miller, ordinarily one of the mildest-mannered of men, scooped up a handful of snow and packed a snowball. While Cook watched open-mouthed, Miller wound up and let fly. The snowball caught LeResche squarely in the forehead, dropping him to his fanny on the cold sidewalk. While LeResche sat sputtering, Cook and Miller were hot-footing it up Front Street under cover of darkness.

ALASKA IS NOT IMMUNE to national trends. Author Dermot Cole described the arrival and local nuances of the streaking phenomenon: [2]

Along with mood rings, pet rocks, and other fads of

the mid-1970s, streakers blazed their way through the pipeline camps. The practice of running naked through public places began on college campuses and had its own anthem, "The Streak," by Ray Stevens.

On the pipeline, the first streakers to be photographed were The Magnificent Seven, a group of men who ran through Atigun Camp, the "Shangri-La of the Trans-Alaska Pipeline," on December 18, 1974.

Shouting "Merry Christmas!" and "Ho-Ho-Ho!" the men followed a route that took them through the warehouse, light truck park, Arctic walkways, and the theater. All this on a thirty-two-below-zero night.

At Galbraith Lake, streakers were required to follow pipeline regulations. There was a streaking roster for the different trades, and prizes for Streaker of the Month, such as a one-week vacation at Prudhoe Bay.

"In a nod to project safety requirements, all streakers are being required to wear bunny boots and hard hats," the *Campfollower* newspaper reported."

GEOFF KENNEDY ONCE worked at a Fairbanks radio station that was affiliated with a television station. The TV outlet was experiencing frequent technical problems, and the result was blank television screens and angry callers.

Geoff began answering the phone by immediately saying: "Thank you for calling the broadcast center. Our engineers are aware of the technical difficulties and are working on correcting the problems as soon as they can. Thanks for your patience."

Through repetition his statement became quite polished, to the point where one caller asked, "Is this a recording?"

Kennedy answered instantly, "Yes, it is."

He then heard the caller turn away from the phone and ask someone, "How do they do that?"

ONE NORTH SLOPE oil worker always left a pair of boots outside his door to differentiate his room from others off the long hallway in the employee housing. One day while he was at work, two of his friends covered his door with aluminum siding that perfectly matched the hallway interior. They placed his boots outside the next room down the hall.

When the man returned at the end of his shift, he found that his key didn't fit the lock, and the room behind his boots was occupied by another worker. He called security to report his room missing. [3]

DAVID COLE RETURNED to his engineering office in Anchorage one April 1 to find that it had disappeared. The former entrance was now simply a wall, nicely painted and covered with framed photos and artwork.

The perpetrators were Cole's co-workers, Tim Potter and Curtis Lapierre. The tables were later turned on Curtis, who arrived one morning to find his office carpet had been replaced with wall-to-wall grass growing in a thriving sod. [4]

ONE DAY MANY YEARS AGO, radio announcer Tom Jensen at KFRB in Fairbanks made a playful announcement to mark the end of summer and arrival of the new season's first freezing temperatures.

He advised newcomers that it was time to change the air in the tires on their cars. That meant getting rid of the warm summer air, which could cause tires to go flat, and replacing it with cold winter air.

Later that day a local service station reported that four different drivers had come in to ask for a change of air.

When a Coast Guard commander insisted the local bawdy houses be closed, the girls announced a close-out sale.

9 | Busy Bodies
True Love, and Other Illusions

The brothels of Ketchikan were on Creek Street, with its row of houses on pilings over Ketchikan Creek. It was said Creek Street was the only place in the world where both fish and fishermen went upstream to spawn.

AN IRS AGENT interviewing Fairbanks hookers was told by Georgia Lee that she had no income to declare. Operating costs like fancy clothes and liquor had eaten up her profits.

"Gee," the agent said, "Panama Hattie has declared $10,000. I would think you'd probably do at least as well."

"Why that old has-been," Georgia snapped. "Put me down for twice that much." [1]

Dolly Arthur was one of the leading ladies of the old Ketchikan red light district on Creek Street. Author June Allen relates this tale about Dolly:

Dolly asked to have the plumbing in her house repaired. The plumber found that several pipes had frozen while Dolly was outside on a vacation and there were several inches of ice on the floor. It was a big mending job.

The plumber said to a friend, "I'm going to fix that girl. The job is a $200 job, but I'm going to make it $265 because she'll kick about the price no matter what it is and then I can come down to $200."

Dolly did indeed grumble about the price, called the plumber a thief and said $265 was an enormous amount for the job.

So he said, "Well, ordinarily I wouldn't think of coming down on a price, but since it's you, Dolly, and we're old friends, I'll ask you: What do you think would be a fair price?"

Dolly pressed her lips together and then said, "I think you should take $15 off the price."

She paid, the plumber recalls, from rolls of bills tucked in her stocking tops and "other parts of her underwear." [2]

DURING WORLD WAR II the commander of the local Coast Guard station demanded that the bawdy houses in Ketchikan be closed. The girls distributed a printed flier announcing a close-out sale.

RON WENDT PASSES ON this story from gold rush days, when flooding washed out several old coffins from a graveyard in a town along the Yukon River. The permafrost had kept the bodies preserved, but no one was quite sure who they were.

Smilin' George was an old timer with a good memory when he was halfway sober, so the townspeople summoned this old gentleman who had spent many years going from gold camp to gold camp searching for his fortune. He was asked to identify the frozen corpses.

George walked up to one of the coffins which happened to have Goldie the dance hall girl frozen in the coffin. The local ladies gathered around to have a look. Smilin' George bent over and looked at the frozen face of the blonde haired woman in the coffin and spoke:

"Well, Goldie, you're still the prettiest girl in town!"

AT KENNY LAKE the weddings can get wild and wooly. One bride wound up getting convicted for assault when she used a .22-caliber revolver in an attempt to shoot a pair of handcuffs off one of the wedding guests. The guest had been demonstrating the cuffs, which were a wedding gift, when he realized nobody had the key. "Bam!" the bride said, describing the disaster. "I missed the handcuff."

A BIG LAKE WOMAN went on the *Geraldo Rivera Show* to talk about the annulment of her two-year marriage. She said she didn't realize her husband was actually a woman.

NOME REINDEER HERDER Chester Seveck once appeared on the old television quiz show "You Bet Your Life," where host Groucho Marx asked him if Eskimos really swap wives. "Yeah," he said, "just like in Hollywood."

KELLIE MCANANY TOOK her visiting parents on a guided fishing trip in Prince William Sound. They were taking a break when Kellie's mom noticed two eagles flying above the boat. The birds would fly apart, then swoop together, seemingly right on top of each other.

What's going on, she asked the guide. He explained that eagles mate in the air.

Kellie's dad, a puckish Irishman from St. Louis, leaned toward his wife and said out of the side of his mouth: "That's what you call flying united."

WHEN MARILYN CROCKETT decided to curtail her career as an Anchorage oil executive to pursue motherhood full time, the choice of words in her letter of resignation may have left something to be desired.

In the letter to Bob Harrison at the Western Oil and Gas Association in Los Angeles, she commented that, "as you know, I'm pregnant."

An uncomfortable Harrison immediately called to congratulate Crockett, at the same time assuring her that he had known nothing about her pregnancy.

STUDENTS AT JUNEAU-DOUGLAS High School wanted to hold a health clinic, but school board members opposed the idea. They worried that the clinic would focus too much on sex. Seniors got even during their graduation ceremony. As they shook hands with the school board representative in the reception line, they palmed off condoms. Then there was the Fairbanks bar that held a Safe Sex Party featuring volleyball using an inflated condom.

FIGHTING FIRES IS ALWAYS challenging, but the ingenuity and audacity of Alaskans sometimes makes all the difference. One day early in the twentieth century, a house fire erupted in Petersburg. The fire department responded but found they had insufficient water for their hoses. The only source was a small stream where the water was so low the pumps wouldn't work.

The homeowner watched glumly until Black Mary, a well-known madam at a Petersburg whorehouse, stripped off her clothes and sat down in the creek, damming it with her body and creating a pool deep enough for the fire pumps. The house was saved.

Black Mary later moved to Ketchikan and became proprietor of the infamous Star, a bawdy house on Creek Street.

A RATHER PASSIONATE elderly woman at the Anchorage Pioneers Home whispered into Ole Peterson's ear, telling him that if he could guess what she had in her hand, he could share her room that night.

Ole, being single but not the brightest light among the pioneers, answered: "An elephant."

She smiled and patted his knee. "That's close enough," she said.

THE ORIGINS OF THIS next piece of verse are obscure, but the energy and spirit of its heroine certainly aren't. It's titled "Tillie from Tok."

I'll tell ye a tall tale of Tillie from Tok.
She mushed far from home with no kale in her poke.
And when she discovered that she'd gone fer broke,
she was fit to be tied, fer it wasn't a joke.

Old hen eggs were sellin' two dollars fer six,
a dollar a piece for small sourdough bricks,
two dollars fer whiskey what mostly was mix.
Poor Tillie was caught in one hell of a fix.

The way it all happened, she strode in a bar.
She ordered a shot and a four-bit cigar.
When a cheechako asked her had she traveled far,
Tillie ordered up drinks fer the whole house, by gar.

Now this Tillie from Tok was the size of a barn,
wore size fourteen shoes and the whole ball of yarn.
A bear or a bull moose gave her no consarn.
She came and she went and she cared not a darn.

Her hair was as red as a spanked baby's head.
With one fingernail she could haul a bobsled.
When horses refuse to be driven or led,
leave the poor beasties rest and drive Tillie instead.

When Tillie decided to be on her way,
the barkeeper hovered nearby fer his pay.
She reached in her poke and turned green with dismay.
Then this cheechako arose and the crowd heard him
*   say:*

"Dear Madam, don't bother your head fer the green.
I've a wad on my hip fair to ransom a queen.
'Tis proud I will be if I might intervene,
for you have the most beautiful hair I have seen."

Now Tillie from Tok sized 'im up fer a spell.
We made sure she'd consign this cheechako to hell.
Instead she stood up and let out a yell,
and hugged this cheechako to a fare-thee-well.

This cheechako was only say four, five foot tall,
while Tillie was built like a brick banquet hall;
about six-foot-four and wide as yon wall.
But love goes where 'tis sent, when once it gets the call.

So she grabbed this cheechako and let out a roar
ye could hear for ten miles as they lit fer the door.
Ye can still see her size fourteen prints in the floor
and that self-same barkeep is still plenty sore.

Bush pilot Don Sheldon didn't even charge extra when he recruited a passenger to hold down a ski tail in midair.

10 | Airheads in Alaska

*Where the Blue Yonder
Is Truly Wild*

*The first time pilot Bob Reeve landed at Shemya in the
Aleutian Islands, known for their fierce winds, he saw
a heavy chain hanging from a pole. "What's that for?"
he asked innocently. "Why," said the ground crewman,
delivering the punch line, "that's our wind sock."*

JOE RYCHETNIK FLEW with many of Alaska's best-
known bush pilots during his years as a state trooper. He
often found himself a passenger in aircraft flown by "Mad
Man" Bill Munz or Ray Decker, a pilot for Munz Northern
Airways. Rychetnik describes Decker as "a gentleman of
the old school but scared to death of Munz and the possi-
bility of losing his job."

Once, flying back from Cape Espenberg and
Shishmaref, I asked Ray if he didn't want to take on
some fuel at Teller, where the trading post kept a few
cases of Chevron for emergencies. He said he had
enough and went on flying for Nome. When we got there,
he pulled his usual stunt of flying down the Nome beach

and buzzing his mobile home before landing at "Munz Field" at the end of the old Municipal Field.

We came in for a very steep landing and stopped at the far end of the field, where the Munz mechanic met us with a pickup truck. I didn't have a chance to ask Ray why we had stopped there instead of at the Munz hangar because he immediately jumped into the back of the pickup to avoid conversation.

We dropped Ray off at the hangar, and I paid the mechanic five dollars to drive me home. On the way in, we talked about the weather and other things, and finally I asked him why Ray stopped the plane out at the far end of the airport.

"Out of gas, my guess!" he said. Ray told me later that Munz didn't like it when he bought gas out of town. [1]

PILOT BOB REEVE eventually became accustomed to the relentless winds of the Aleutian Island chain. Author Beth Day writes: "The turbulent air through which he flew daily was such a normal condition that it became routine."

On one flight in from the Chain, after being socked in for a full week and living on Army rations, Reeve hit the usual patch of violent air in Lake Clark Pass, fought his way through and landed at Anchorage. When they were safely down, one of his passengers said to Reeve, "In civilian life I am a psychologist. And I couldn't help but be curious as to just what was going through your mind when we were being tossed around in that violent air. Would you tell me?"

Reeve scratched his head and thought back. "Oh, I remember. I was wondering what my wife was going to give me for lunch." [2]

AFTER EXPERIENCING AN ONBOARD gunfight between two drunken passengers, pilot Bob Reeve developed his own means of dealing with passengers who tipple aloft. Beth Day writes:

> From then on, Bob "frisked" his passengers and took away all their guns, knives and booze. . . .
>
> To fool Reeve, the workers began stringing pints of liquor inside their pants, from their belts. Reeve missed this for a while—till he heard one of the men bragging; then he began frisking for that bottle too.
>
> "I didn't much like bending over to inspect their legs—and leaving my head and back defenseless," says Reeve, "so I asked Bill Borland (six-foot, three-inches; 220 pounds) to stand behind me. I always had a feeling they'd jump me like a bunch of wolves when I bent over—but they never did with Bill standing there looking like a ton of granite." [3]

BUSH PILOT DON SHELDON went to the rescue in a notable incident that certainly had its humorous side.

Sheldon got involved after a pilot staggered into the airport at Talkeetna and reported that his plane had crash-landed in the Talkeetna River during takeoff.

"After the plane hit, it was all I could do to get out of it," the pilot told Sheldon. "I swam to shore, and when I looked back, it was too dark to see anything. I don't know if the passengers got out or not. I hope to God they haven't drowned."

Aboard were two passengers, including the jolly, red-haired owner of the Fairbanks Hotel, a woman of ample girth. Sheldon got a helper and flew off in his Super Cub to find the wreck. Author James Greiner picks up the story at this point:

> As they neared the area the pilot had described,

this is our Son-in-Laws Dad.

Sheldon stared in disbelief through the fingers of rain that fanned upward across the windscreen in the prop wash of the Super Cub. On a narrow sandbar in the middle of the river, jumping up and down and waving her arms frantically, was the huge proprietress of the Fairbanks Hotel.

What made the sight totally incongruous to Sheldon was the fact that she was "naked as a jaybird and resembled a white elephant. One thing that could be said—she would have been hard to miss, even in the poor light of a rainy morning. She was waving her clothes at us, and after recovering from our surprise, we made three passes over the tiny sandbar. It was only about 10 feet wide and 30 feet long, and Pedro managed a direct hit with only one sleeping bag. The food and the other bags ended up in the river."

Sheldon then made the short hop back to Talkeetna, landing at 5:30 a.m. The light was getting better, but it was still too dark to land the floatplane on the river.

"At 7:30, the weather had improved and we took off. Again we overflew the sandbar a couple of times, and I decided to land on the stretch of river above the stranded woman, because of the current and the sharp bend downriver. Once on the water, I had to taxi backward downstream to get her."

Over the slipstream of the idling Continental engine, the woman wailed, "I'm sure damned glad to see you."

Her teeth chattered between blue lips, and she had the wet sleeping bag loosely draped over her ample shoulders.

"Hop aboard, and we'll have ya back in Talkeetna in a shake."

On their arrival, Sheldon happily learned that the third member of the fishing party had staggered into town after wandering all night through the wet mosquito-infested brush.

Back in the Fairview Inn, still wearing the sleeping bag at half-mast and nothing else, the big woman from Fairbanks bought drinks all around. [4]

AN OLD STORY SAYS that a woman phoned down from her hotel room in Fairbanks to tell the proprietor that a bush pilot was molesting her.

"How do you know it's a bush pilot?" asked the proprietor.

"He's got high boots, a watch with seven hands, and a nickel in his pants pocket." [5]

WRITER JOE RYCHETNIK tells a funny tale about pilot Archie Ferguson:

Ferguson had another adventure the day he flew a load of freight from Nome to the Native village of Elim, east of Nome on Norton Sound. Archie was afraid the Elim airstrip might be muddy because the winter snow and ice were breaking up but the long, dry summer days hadn't yet arrived. He ran into an Eskimo from Elim who was working in Nome and asked how the airstrip was.

"Pilot land there last week," the villager told him.

Archie loaded his Cessna bush plane and took off for Elim, not a very long flight. The weather was great, and he could see the field clearly. It looked a bit soggy to him, so he went around and looked it over again at a lower elevation. For some reason, he decided it was OK to land. He said to himself that if the other pilot landed there, he certainly could.

The wheels of his plane dug furrows in the mud before they quickly stopped rolling, and the Cessna turned over on its back. Archie was not happy. After unloading the plane and repairing the damage, he flew back to Nome and sought out the man from Elim who had given him the bum advice.

"I landed there and my plane turned over on its back!" Archie complained to the villager.

The Eskimo replied, "Other pilot do same thing." [6]

BUSH PILOT DON SHELDON was once hired by three church administrators from Ohio who wanted to visit church missions around Talkeetna and to see wildlife and scenery along the way.

"During the long well-lit hours of this particular day," Joe Rychetnik writes, "Don moved the churchmen from village to village, always via some great spectacle like Mount McKinley gleaming up over the clouds or the striped backs of the glaciers flowing down from the giant mountain."

Then Sheldon treated the business-suited churchmen to overflights of moose, grizzly bears, and caribou. He topped off the flight by landing his Cessna where the visitors could photograph the animals up close. Rychetnik continues:

All the cameras were empty when Don loaded the churchmen back aboard and headed the silver plane into the wind. The bumpy takeoff was more than a bit of bush field inconvenience. It concealed the fact that a bungee cord that held the front tip of a landing ski in position had broken. . . .

With the right-front bungee broken and the plane in the air, there was a grave situation that could mean a possibly deadly crash on landing. The ski, now flying flat against the slipstream and held that way by the rear bungee, was making the plane very unstable. Don had to keep full power on, causing the plane to roar as if in a permanent takeoff. Staying aloft was becoming problematical.

Don, not wanting to add alarm to the bad situation, turned around to look at the passengers and told them, "Gentlemen, we are going too slow to fly and too fast to crash. We will not be able to land unless we can get the ski down. How about you"—and he pointed to the man seated next to the right-hand door in the back seat—"getting out on the tail of the ski."

This order met with dumb looks. But Don poked around with his free hand, found an end of a mountaineering rope, and told the unhappy prospect to tie the rope around his waist. Don told the man to zip up his jacket and put on his gloves; he was going out to counterbalance the errant ski.

The other passengers held on to their partner as he pushed his legs out the door, fighting the slipstream. Don tied the other end of the rope to a seat belt, hoping its strength would not have to be tested.

Luckily the man had galoshes on to protect his feet and lower legs, and the partially closed door sheltered most of him from the icy slipstream. He was now partway in and partway out of the plane. He floundered around with his feet until he found the edge of the ski tail and then, lowering his weight, he slowly brought the tip down to near horizontal. The Cessna immediately began to fly better, and all aboard realized that the sacrifice in comfort had to be made for all their safety. . . . The fellow on the ski tail could not be relieved, and he hung there, partially in and partially out of the plane, for nearly ninety minutes while Don raced for home. . . . The plane settled firmly to the airstrip on its skis, and the horror of balancing the ski tip was over. The nearly frozen passenger was soon thawed.

This remarkable chapter in Rychetnik's book was aptly entitled "Missionary's Position." [7]

"FLYING INTO THE HANDSOME new 7,500-foot runway at Nome," writes Beth Day, "Jim Dodson hit a thirty-mile crosswind and, electing to land with the wind rather than against it, calmly set his plane down across the 500-foot width of the runway, directly in front of the tower.

"Army personnel in the tower scattered, sure the 'wild man' would crash into the building. But the CAA control man laughed.

"'He knows what he's doing. He's been landing on 500-foot fields all his life.'"

RAY TREMBLAY KNEW it would be dark when he arrived at the 1,500-foot unlighted airstrip at Paxson, so he took an important precaution. He asked a worker to put a gas lantern on the exact end of the usable runway on the left-hand corner, as a guide for his descent and landing.

As anticipated, it was quite dark when I returned and after several passes, the lantern appeared and finally became stationary at the end of the field.

I made a long approach with my eyes on the lantern, came up even with it, chopped the power and hauled back on the stick ready for touchdown. Suddenly, a sickening, sinking sensation surged through me as the bottom fell out. The airplane stalled and plunged for what felt like an eternity before hitting the ground.

Needless to say, what was supposed to be a featherlight landing turned into a bone-jarring, soul-quaking crash, which would have destroyed the landing gear on any airplane but that of the gullwing. After gingerly bringing the plane to a halt and finding out how many teeth I had left, if any, I shakily walked back to find out what had happened.

Nothing much, except for the fact that my young friend had really wanted to help me out. To do so, he had attached the gas lantern, my handsome guiding light, to a twenty-foot pole which he had then proudly held high into the air above his head. [8]

RAY TREMBLAY CONFESSES to a classic embarrassing moment on the day he was flying a group of wildlife experts from Fairbanks to observe a caribou herd.

After everyone was settled, I cranked up the engine and allowed it to warm up as I monitored the gauges. Since my passengers were not pilots I was naturally going to impress them with my flying skills, so I activated the switch making all radio transmissions audible on the overhead speaker. . . .

After everything was ready, I called the tower in my most professional voice, "Fairbanks tower this is Stinson N782 parked in front of the tower and ready to taxi."

The operator answered, "N782 cleared to taxi to runway 19, wind calm, suggest you untie your wings first." [9]

No luxury car for Governor Tony Knowles during a D.C. snowstorm. He drove to the White House in a Ford Explorer.

11 | Our Fearless Leaders

Good Government? Good Grief!

Former governor Jay Hammond said it: "With our small population, virtually any idiot who aspires to public office is likely to get elected."

IN 1958, WHEN CAMPAIGNING for one of Alaska's first two seats in the U.S. Senate, Ernest Gruening met an elderly man on an Anchorage street who said, "I'd sooner vote for the devil."

"Well," Gruening responded, "I admit he'd be a very formidable opponent. But if he chooses not to run, would you consider me?"

Gruening said the man responded, "You son of a bitch, I might just do that."

THE LATE BOB BARTLETT, former delegate to Congress from the Alaska Territory and later U.S. senator, had a well-known sense of humor. Here's Bartlett's version of what he did on March 1, 1954, as he was about to enter the House chamber just as Puerto Rican nationalists began shooting.

"I gave some thought to dashing into the fray and capturing whoever was doing the shooting, but decided to reflect on that a bit further and, in order to establish the proper atmosphere for thinking, moved behind a nearby and very thick pillar. I had been there quite briefly when the limited space became extremely crowded and the boys started to shove me aside."

The doors of the House chamber "just then opened and numerous House members came galloping out seeking safety. Most everyone who had been in the vicinity later claimed credit for capturing one or more of the shooters. I would have been in on the kill too, finally, if I had not been required to stop and tie a shoelace." [1]

GOVERNOR STEVE COWPER visited Kotzebue in 1989 during a tour of Alaska National Guard posts. Cowper felt uncomfortable wearing a jacket and tie in Kotzebue, so he decided to honor the Guardsmen by donning their military fatigues uniform. The governor was accompanied by a plainclothes state trooper, a distinguished-looking officer who wore a suit. As the two men emerged from the Nullagvik Hotel, got into a car, and headed for the airport, a tourist turned to reporter Lin Gale of the *Fairbanks Daily News-Miner* and said: "I heard the governor of Alaska was here, but why is he driving that soldier around?"

JAY HAMMOND IS ONE of the most colorful people ever to make his home in the Alaskan wilderness. Hammond has been a Marine fighter pilot, a government hunter, a trapper, guide, bush pilot, legislator, and eventually governor of Alaska. He likes to tell it straight. Here are a few quotes from his autobiography, *Tales of Alaska's Bush Rat Governor:* [2]

"So long as you state something in bold, obscure, confident terms, chances are most folk will believe you. . . .

Some of the most physically and mentally bereft candidates captivate voters by asserting inanities in stentorian tones."

"Hammond's Law Number One: *The abundance of discourse is inversely proportionate to the significance of the subject.*

"Hammond's Law Number Two: *The number of sides to a given issue is double the sum of the square of the number of attorneys debating it.*"

Referring to Alaska Independence Party Leader Joe Vogler: "Anyone who can come up with language like 'posey sniffing swine' can't be all bad."

Responding to a reporter who wanted to know why Teamsters leader Jesse Carr had called Hammond an SOB: "Jesse and I were both Marines, but I didn't think he thought we had anything else in common."

ASKED BY JIMMY CARTER what kind of plane he flew, Hammond told the president about his single-engine 1953 Cessna 170.

"Don't Alaskans worry about you flying around by yourself in an ancient aircraft like that?" Carter asked

"No," Hammond said. "In fact, I'm encouraged by many to do so. During my campaign, Jesse Carr's Teamsters even offered to contribute a hundred gallons of aviation gas, and throw the sugar in free."

QUESTIONED ON HIS VIEWS on a proposed atomic test, Hammond told a reporter it was abominable even to consider an atomic blast on an island where remnant species of endangered sea otters are found.

"If they must use an island location for their test, they should at least find one where the indigenous species aren't endangered," Hammond said.

We all played Tennis in the same place. Dr. Gould putted his teeth.

Lives Across from Homer.

"Do you have such an island in mind?" the reporter asked.
"Certainly. Why not Manhattan?"

JAY HAMMOND TELLS how State Representative
Wendell Kay, an Anchorage attorney, once castigated a
colleague, Clem Tillion. Kay criticized Tillion for taking his
shoes off during legislative sessions and for failing to stand
when addressing the chair. Kay even suggested that the
location of Clem's brain prevented it from functioning prop-
erly when constrained by shoe leather.

In his laconic reply, Tillion seemed to accept Kay's theory:
"Brain location is indeed a primary consideration; to
function fully, one's gray matter must not be subjected to
undue pressure. This, of course, is why barristers must
stand when they speak."

HERE'S HOW JAY HAMMOND recalls a roll call vote
in the state Senate as the Speaker called out each name:
"Devaugh?" "Aye."
"Hammond?" "Aye."
"Kendall?" "Aye."
"Rader?" "Aye."
"Sweeney?" "Aye."
"Tillion?" Silence. Again, louder:
"Tillion?" No response.
"Mister Tillion!"
"Uhh? Here!"
"No, Mr. Tillion, we're voting on House Bill Fifty-six,
not recording who's present. You've already established
your *absence*. Now let's have your vote."

GOVERNOR TONY KNOWLES once arrived in Washington, D.C., during a midwinter snowstorm, on his way to a function at the White House. He took one look at the luxury car that had been rented for him and decided to trade it for a less ostentatious Ford Explorer.

When the governor's driver asked if he really wanted to go to the White House in the smaller vehicle, Knowles looked around at the cars spinning in the snow, then replied: "Hey, it'll be easier to push through the gate than a Cadillac."

STATE REPRESENTATIVE RAMONA BARNES received an especially nasty letter from a new constituent in her district, demanding that the marijuana laws be liberalized. Offended by the tone of the letter, Barnes worked out her anger by sitting down at a typewriter and pounding out her "dream answer," as follows:

Thank you for contacting me so soon after moving into my district. After close examination of your letter and your assessment of my record as a legislator, I have come to the conclusion that one of us has got to go. Since it won't be me, I suggest that you strongly consider moving to a more compatible district where bleeding hearts and greenies live on in blissful ignorance, surrounded by parks, greenbelts and waist-high marijuana plants. Best wishes for a speedy relocation.

Feeling much better, she signed the letter with a flourish and set it aside, intending to show it to a colleague before throwing it in the trash.

But a member of her staff came into the office later. Seeing the signed letter, the conscientious staffer typed out an envelope and sent the missive on its way. The impact on its recipient is unknown, but a copy of the letter made its way into the pages of an Anchorage newspaper.

It was tough to prosecute a rape case in which one of the defendant's hands was on a thigh, the other on a piece of pie.

12 | Justice Alaska-style
Disorder in Court

The defendant, serving as his own lawyer during a criminal trial in Anchorage, called his former girlfriend as a witness.
Defendant: *"Isn't it true that you dumped me and stopped visiting me in jail?"*
Witness: *"I quit seeing you because you told me you were guilty. You're a lying scumbag and you know it."*
Defendant: *"No more questions."*

A HEAVILY MUSCLED Anchorage man who was periodically arrested for small offenses had an aversion to handcuffs, often becoming violent when police tried to use them. Most officers knew about the man's oddity. They knew that if they let him climb into the police cruiser without handcuffs, he would come along peacefully.

One new officer decided they were being too lenient with the man. When the time came, this officer went to the man's house, placed him under arrest, and tried to force cuffs on him.

The man fought briefly, then picked the officer up and threw him through a wall. The officer picked himself up from atop a pile of sheetrock and broken wall studs in the next room, then stooped and stepped back through the wall.

"OK," he said with a sigh of resignation, "no cuffs. What else, you want to drive the cruiser?"

OFFICER JOSEPH YOUNG was manning the Anchorage Police Department's complaint desk, which often heard from drivers who wanted to gripe about policemen who had ticketed them. Oftentimes the complainants didn't have the officer's name or badge number, so they were asked for a description or some distinguishing characteristic. One senior officer, for example, was missing a number of teeth on one side of his mouth, causing his cheek to pooch in slightly.

One complainant tried to describe an officer with a description that wasn't particularly helpful: "older, tall, thin . . . " Then a light came on in his eyes; he had thought of the perfect identifier: "This dude," the man said, "he looks like he's been smoking dynamite." Young knew instantly who it was.

ANCHORAGE LAWYER Wayne Anthony Ross once defended a man accused of hitting a woman in the face with a piece of pie. In his formal response to the district attorney, Ross proposed that the case be resolved with a showdown on an Anchorage street corner.

The man and woman would confront each other, with the woman to be armed with the pie of her choice. She would be given a free throw. Ross would serve as his client's "second" and the district attorney would do the honors for the woman.

The offer wasn't accepted, but the district attorney dismissed the case.

A JUROR, ABOUT TO BE sworn in to hear the case of a state representative charged with owning illegal guns, was asked if she was acquainted with the defendant. She said she had known him her entire life. In fact, she said, "he put my hand in a washing machine wringer when I was four."

The judge asked her if she was still mad at the man. Not at all, she said. "I even voted for him." (The legislator was acquitted.)

JOE RYCHETNIK, an Alaska trooper back in the early days of statehood, claims the repeat offenders in his district actually looked forward to occasional short stays in the Nome jail. After all, they had three meals a day, dental care, movies every night, and a chance to renew old friendships.

The lack of lockups in smaller communities meant prisoners either had to be watched constantly until they could be moved to Nome or trusted to show up when the bush plane arrived to transport them. On one occasion the plane arrived early at a stop and Rychetnik saw his prisoner come running toward the airstrip, afraid he would miss his trip to Nome.

AFTER ARRESTING AN ACCUSED murderer in Unalakleet, Rychetnik handcuffed the prisoner to a chair in a heated storeroom because they wouldn't be able to fly out until the next day. Rychetnik hired two young men to watch the prisoner, and he gave them the key to the handcuffs so the man could take toilet breaks.

Next morning Rychetnik went to the storeroom with coffee and sweet rolls, but both his prisoner and the guards were missing. When he found the guards, they told him the prisoner, their brother-in-law, had hypnotized them into letting him go. The prisoner was found later in the day, visiting friends.

LAWYER M. ASHLEY DICKERSON filed a document in 1980 that quickly became a classic in Alaska jurisprudence:

COUNTERCLAIM

As a counterclaim against plaintiff, defendant would show unto the court as follows:

That defendant counterclaimant is a minor and a student. That defendant had always enjoyed a good reputation in his community and peer group.

That on divers occasions during the months of January and February, 1980, the plaintiff wantonly, maliciously with an intent to damage defendant and to lower his standards in his peer group made the following slanderous remarks against defendant specifically, "Stan eats pussy." That said remark was false and plaintiff knew same to be false but made same for the purpose of embarrassing and humiliating defendant.

That said remark received wide publicity and did cause humiliation and embarrassment to defendant much to his damage in a sum in excess of $10,000 to be proved at the time of trial.

WHEREFORE defendant prays for damages against the plaintiff in a sum in excess of $10,000 to be proved at the time of trial, costs and attorney's fees and all other relief right and proper in the premises.

Dated at Anchorage, Alaska this 21st day of July, 1980

M. ASHLEY DICKERSON, INC.
Attorney for the Defendant,
Counterclaimant

THE FEDERAL PROSECUTOR, trying a rape case in Juneau, slowly and somberly asked the victim: "Annie, what happened that night?"

"We were sitting on the dock," she said, "and he put his hand on my leg."

Very dramatically, the prosecutor asked: "What happened next?"

"He put his hand near my tummy," she answered.

Sensing the shock value of the moment, the prosecutor followed with: "What was he doing with the other hand?"

"He was eating a piece of pie," she said. [1]

YEARS AGO, *Anchorage Daily News* outdoor columnist Slim Randles sued the competing *Anchorage Times* for libel.

The reason for the suit is probably best left unremembered, but those who worked at the *Times* will never forget the trial itself.

The *Times* staff watched each morning as Slim entered the courthouse across the street, then waited until late afternoon to hear a verbal account of the day's happenings from the reporter covering the trial.

Slim was a colorful man who refused to hire a lawyer, making his own arguments and using distinctively non-legal language to express his outrage and pain. Members of the *Times* staff were anxiously aware that Slim seemed truly angry.

On the last day of the trial, Slim parked in his usual spot near the courthouse. But this time he emerged from his pickup carrying a shotgun. Instead of heading for the courthouse, Slim strode purposefully toward the *Times* office.

Editors and reporters watched his approach in horror, then dove for cover when he appeared in the newsroom door, the shotgun cradled in his arms.

Slim looked around at the rapidly emptying newsroom in growing confusion. He looked down at the shotgun, realized what everyone was thinking, and shouted in terror: "Marnie, come get your goddamned gun."

My wife, Marnie, was the only person in the room who hadn't ducked under a desk. She sat with her head in her hands, wishing fervently she had not agreed to buy the shotgun from Slim. It was to be a surprise present for my birthday.

Slim had decided that since he had to drive in to

Anchorage that day anyway, it would be a good time to deliver my present.

POLICE OFFICER JOSEPH YOUNG was on duty for the Anchorage Police Department early one beautiful summer Sunday when a call came over his car radio about a heart attack victim. Young arrived at the house just as another patrol car pulled up and a sergeant and a detective jumped out.

The men rushed to the door and knocked loudly. No response. They pounded again, and still no answer. Young said the victim could be unconscious. The sergeant and the detective stepped back, ran at the door, and kicked it in, knocking it inward and out of its frame. The door landed on the hallway floor in a cloud of dust, sheetrock, and wood splinters.

Within seconds a wide-eyed and obviously terrified man ran from a bedroom in his underwear, trying desperately to pull on a pair of pants. He hopped clumsily up the hall, dragging his pants, bobbing awkwardly toward the three large men looming in his hallway.

"Are you having a heart attack?" the sergeant asked.

"I wasn't," the man said. "But I am now."

The supposed victim lived in the house next door. And he had been drunk, not suffering a heart attack. The city of Anchorage gave his neighbor a new door and an apology.

Some criminals have a terrible sense of timing. FBI Agent John Jensen encountered one while investigating a robbery at a bank in the Muldoon neighborhood of Anchorage.

Jensen was at the bank, showing photographs of suspects to a teller. The teller was at her counter, still on duty, so Jensen stepped aside to allow a customer to go up to her.

Shortly after the customer stepped to the counter, Jensen saw a frightened look on the teller's face. She handed a stack of money to the man, who then headed for the exit.

Jensen followed him to the door, then disarmed and arrested him, thus setting an Alaska record for response time to a robbery and collaring of the crook.

A MAN IDENTIFYING HIMSELF as "Jeff" dialed a wrong number and got the Anchorage Police Department drug unit by mistake. When a man answered, Jeff immediately began talking about how much he had enjoyed the previous night's party and all the pot smoking.

Finally he asked: "Is Nick there?"

"No," answered the police officer. "I'm Bill."

The conversation continued and Jeff offered to sell Bill some cocaine. Sgt. Bill Miller then recruited some backup and went to Jeff's house to make the drug buy. Jeff and two other men went to jail.

ANOTHER CRIMINAL GENIUS donned a ski mask and charged into the lobby of the Holiday Inn in downtown Anchorage during a police training conference.

"Gimme all your money and you won't get hurt," he told the desk clerk. The clerk handed the robber a stack of bills and watched wide-eyed as the masked man ran for the door. Midway across the lobby he was tackled by a team of rather large officers.

"As soon as we hit him, money was flying in the air, just like in the cartoons," said Juneau Police Sgt. Steve Hernandez.

Hotel manager Stephen Horton said the robber was "definitely a candidate for America's dumbest criminal."

Hot dogs and hand grenades—they're just part of "urban fishing" in the shadows of Anchorage's sky scrapers.

13 | Fish and Games

Humans Versus the Other Animals

A Fairbanks doctor asked the patient, a trapper, about the large scar on his nether parts. The man explained he had been setting traps, chaining them into position, when he answered the call of nature and inadvertently tripped a chained trap.
"Doc, that was the second most painful experience of my life," the trapper said.
"What was the first?"
"When I hit the end of that chain."

MY GOOD FRIEND Harvey Rayner, visiting from Massachusetts, needed an Alaska fishing license, so we stopped at a small general store that handled them. Harvey filled out the forms, but when it came time to pay, he realized that his traveler's checks were in a pouch on a belt wrapped around his midsection. The pouch was inside his trousers and up against his backside.

He quietly asked the store proprietor if she had a bathroom or storeroom where he could get to his money belt.

By this time a sizable line of other customers had formed behind him.

The woman said no room was available. So Harvey shrugged, dropped his pants, and fished the traveler's checks from their hiding place. The people in line roared with laughter. A red-faced Harvey rearranged his trousers and paid, while apologizing to the proprietor.

She laughed heartily. "The pleasure's all mine," she said.

LARRY EDFELT SHOWED a sympathetic understanding of the quirks of the Alaskan sportfisherman in his columns for the *Juneau Empire*.

"Over the years," he once wrote, "great minds have brooded about whether fishermen were crazier than golfers."

There is much to be said for both sides. Golfers spend hours knocking an innocent little ball across the landscape, often getting wet and numb in the process, and return home with nothing to show for their efforts. Fishermen, on the other hand, spend hours dragging an innocent herring through the water, often getting wet and numb in the process, and return home with nothing to show for their efforts.

On successful days in both sports, joy reigns supreme because the participant has triumphed through enormous skill, but at least the fisherman's rush comes from outsmarting something that has a nervous system.

EDFELT POINTED OUT in another column that:

Salmon fishing with electronics can be mastered by any man, woman, or child of average intelligence, ability and inherited money. Electronic fishing aids are a sound investment. Spending several thousand dollars for a good system has enhanced the resale value of my boat by $600.

At day's end, when I'm back in the harbor snapping photos of dead fish caught by virtue of my considerable steely-eyed, seafaring wisdom, I try not to think about the fact that every one of those salmon I and thousands of dollars worth of electronic intelligence collaborated to outsmart has a brain smaller than a pencil eraser.

EDFELT SCOOPED THE WORLD when he unveiled the Alaska Department of Fish and Game's new salmon allocation plan for Southeast Alaska:

50 percent to gillnetters.

50 percent to purse seiners.

50 percent to trollers.

Remainder to sport fishing.

PROMOTER STEVE SHEPHERD tells of a fishing trip on Sucker Creek north of Anchorage with his pals Michael Cardenas and Michael Kavakob. Shepherd and Kavakob caught their limits of king salmon while Cardenas was left with nothing but frustration. Eventually he tied into a large fish, played it as it tore through the creek's shallow waters, and proudly hoisted it onto the grass.

While Shepherd and Kavakob congratulated him, Cardenas watched in horror as his hard-won fish flopped free and shot back into the creek. Cardenas jumped in after the fish, splashed behind it, and dove football-style onto its back. He wrapped his arms around the fish and clung tight, then hugged it fiercely as he worked his way on elbows and knees back to the bank. He climbed onto shore, the fish clamped in his arms, to cheers from his companions.

A FISH PROCESSING SHIP with multiple owners sank in the Bering Sea in 1990. The controlling owners decided that the sinking and the subsequent insurance proceeds were the legal equivalent of a sale and that they deserved an $800,000 commission for the transaction.

SOLITARY ANGLING ON PRISTINE waters is only one kind of fishing. There's also what Alaskans call "combat fishing"—standing rod-to-rod with others in pursuit of salmon. And when it's done on Ship Creek in Anchorage, it goes by the more genteel name "urban fishing."

No words describe it better. Ship Creek flows through downtown, and urban fishers ply their hobby in the shadow of skyscrapers. "Two blocks from the heart of Anchorage, king salmon weighing fifty pounds or more are available for the plucking in mid-summer," writes Lew Freedman. "Fifteen-story buildings mark the skyline, horns beep from backed-up traffic congestion, but in the midst of the hurly-burly of big-city life is a nearly idyllic, pastoral scene. Albeit a crowded scene."

The annual Ship Creek Salmon Derby brings ten days of competition and a festival atmosphere. "Determined fishermen fish, vendors with hot dog carts set up shop, derby officials sell souvenirs," Freedman writes. "There are pins, buttons, and T-shirts for sale commemorating each year's event and one slightly daffy inventor offers the ultimate souvenir for close-quarters fishing: a real (though defused) multicolored hand grenade, pin still attached.

[handwritten marginal note: GeT TRApped iN mud. "OuR driNKiNg wATeR".]

"This is the ultimate for making your own space."

Freedman tells about two men walking along the section of creek with the most fishermen. One man checked his watch, worried that the vendors might be about to close up shop.

"Got to get my hot dog and hand grenade," he said. [1]

ONE OF FISHING GUIDE Gary Galbraith's clients, a woman in her sixties, had to go to the bathroom.

"There are the bushes," Galbraith told her.

Lew Freedman relates the rest of the story:

The woman discreetly stepped out of sight, into the brush, dropped her trousers, and relieved herself. Just as she pulled up her pants, she let out a squeal and came running out of the trees.

Was there a bear chasing her? Some other wild animal? Sort of. There was a man lying in the brush.

Turns out, it was a state fish and game agent trying to be invisible. He was wearing a camouflage outfit and was in position to spy on fishermen flouting the law. He didn't want to blow his cover, and when the woman squatted just about on top of him, he figured the best thing to do was stay quiet and out of sight.

"She tinkled pretty near right on top of him," said Galbraith. "He was so embarrassed, he didn't move."

Until she screamed.

That was the end of the man toughing it out. The guy stood up and sheepishly said, "Hi, Gary."

A year later, Galbraith brought a different load of people to the same island for a routine snack and break. That time Galbraith actually spotted the same agent lying in the bushes and casually announced loudly to the group that he had to go to the bathroom. Galbraith began walking right to the spot where the man was hidden. No trying to lay low this time. He popped up and said to Galbraith, "Don't even think about it." [2]

THE OPENING LINE of the recipe for Yankee Bob's Fruit-Stuffed Grouse: "For each person to be served, find, then head-shoot, one grouse." [3]

ANCHORAGE ATTORNEY and sometimes-candi-date-for-governor Wayne Anthony Ross was once stuck in a cabin on the Naknek River, waiting out the bad weather for a chance to hunt caribou. Ross and his two partners, Bob Griffin and Jerry Yelter, played poker for two days and were thoroughly bored.

"When do you think we'll be able to get out and hunt?" Ross asked Yelter.

Just then, Yelter spotted a mouse running across the floor and into a rubber raft stored at the rear of the cabin.

"How about now?" Yelter answered. "And I'll guaran-tee you a shot."

Ross bet Yelter a thousand dollars that he could bring down his prey. Ross unloaded the bullets from a Colt pis-tol and inserted a special load containing bird shot, then cocked the hammer.

Yelter jumped into the raft and out came the mouse, running down a rope and across the floor. Ross pulled the trigger but heard only a "click." He had forgotten that a Colt chamber revolves to the right, unlike his customary

Smith & Wesson. He had put the bird shot into the wrong chamber.

Later that evening, the mouse crawled under the cabin again and was seen sneaking back into the raft.

"Do you want to try again?" Yelter asked. "It'll cost you another thousand."

Ross nodded and reloaded the Colt.

Yelter jumped into the raft and the mouse again came darting out, then paused in the middle of the floor. Ross took aim and pulled the trigger. This time the big pistol roared, but then things went bad.

The bird-shot shell contained insufficient gunpowder. The bird-shot canister was supposed to break up in the pistol's barrel, allowing the shot to spread before it reached its target. The low load of powder caused the canister to remain intact, hitting behind the mouse and tearing a large hole in the carpet.

At that point the canister disintegrated and the bird shot bounced off the floor, hit the walls, and ricocheted through the cabin. The pellets hit everything in the room except the mouse. Nobody was injured, but Ross endured howls and catcalls from his hunting partners and had to surrender another thousand dollars to Yelter.

Air fare provided for the ideal bouncer: 6'8" or over, ugly, tough and mean, but diplomatic, weight 280-300 lbs.

14 | Indoor Sports

Bellies Up to the Bar

Chilkoot Charlie's saloon in Anchorage has its motto emblazoned across the outside wall of its building: "We Cheat the Other Guy and Pass the Savings on to You."

THE WALLS AND CEILING of the famous Bird House bar near Anchorage were so heavily papered with driver's licenses, business cards, bits of underwear, and other mementos left by patrons that it was said to be the only bar in Alaska you could hold up with a Zippo.

It was actually a fire that was the final undoing of the Bird House. "By the time crews doused the blaze, the landmark was reduced to a steaming charcoal hulk." the *Anchorage Daily News* reported after the 1996 fire.

Gone were generations of business cards, some inscribed with their owners' physical measurements. Gone were the assorted props and gimmicks—the boneless chickens, stinky pickles and raunchy postcards—that amused or suckered tourists and guests from out of town. Gone, too, was the infamous "ptarmigan call"; blow hard into the horn and coat your face with flour.

Bird House patron Steve Duggan reminisced: "I

remember coming in here once and there was a topless woman standing right there next to the bird, getting her picture taken, like it was nothing. Then she came in and ordered a drink."

That was not so unusual, according to bartender Jan Berkhahn: "We had nineteen and a half nude people in here once in the '80s."

AT THE PEAK of construction on the trans-Alaska pipeline, a Valdez nightclub took out this ad in a Seattle newspaper:

Tavern Bouncer person wanted. Must be 6'8" or over, ugly, tough and mean, but diplomatic, pref. 280-300 lbs. The bigger, the better. $50 shift, room and board. Will pay air fare to Valdez, Alaska. [1]

A BAR OVER ON Fourth Street in Anchorage has a sign that boasts, "The only difference between this place and the *Titanic* is that they had a band."

"THE GREAT THING about Alaska is that you don't need any training, education, talent, or intelligence to succeed," says the humorist known as Mr. Whitekeys. "People will pay you huge amounts of money for doing something you don't know how to do. It's fabulous."

Two weeks after I arrived in Anchorage, an ad for a piano player appeared in the paper. I had never played piano. I played guitar and organ, so what the heck, I answered the ad. Within days I was the band's new piano player at Chilkoot Charlie's. They called Chilkoot's a "rustic Alaskan saloon." A tourist from California once said it a little different: "Rustic—hell! The place is a dump!"

The interior was like a log cabin with the bark still on the logs. There were peanuts on each table in every kind of container imaginable: gold pans, hard hats, and even bedpans. The floor was 3 inches deep in what looked like sawdust, except it really wasn't sawdust: it was crushed peanut shells, which they only swept up twice a year.

This ensured two things—great atmosphere and a very healthy mouse population. After closing the bar at 5 a.m., the bartenders sometimes actually took out their guns and went mouse hunting. Things are a lot different today. The bars close at 3 a.m.

The band played in a small piano bar. Behind us was a fake log wall and the audience sat just across the piano. You got so that you could instantly recognize a certain kind of terrified expression on their faces— their eyes bugged out, their mouths dropped open, and sometimes they pointed at the wall. It was a signal that the mice were running across the logs on the back wall of the stage. You never knew if they were screaming for you or screaming because of the mice.

It was probably the latter, because we were awful. We played a lot of blues. There's an old musicians' saying: "I like the blues 'cause when the record wears out, the music still sounds the same." The trio started out with Friendly Don on bass and a fired air traffic controller named Davey Fitz on drums. We eventually evolved into a racially tolerant band composed of an Arab, a Jew, and a real estate salesman. . . .

The band played at Chilkoot Charlie's for five years, but nobody realized it. Every week we took a new Polaroid picture and ran it in the club's newspaper ad, giving the same band a different name. People would come in every week and complain that we weren't as good as the band that was there last week. Drinking in moderation was a concept that hadn't arrived in Alaska. [2]

Our Area

MR. WHITEKEYS ALSO wrote a classic description of Anchorage's Spenard neighborhood: [3]

Spenard is the sleaziest part of Anchorage. It's filled with bars, strip joints, liquor stores, and massage parlors. A 1957 ad heralded the appearance of La-Wanda, the Flame Goddess, at the Club Mambo. Nothing has changed.

There's the office of a dentist named Dr. Paine. There's PJ's, "A strip joint, but it's a class strip joint." There's a pawn shop with a portable sign that once advertised a Mother's Day special on ammo. There's a massage parlor with a portable sign that announced PLAYMATES, until someone removed the L. It's now been nearly a year and the sign still reads PAYMATES.

Spenard is more than a town—it's a state of mind. It's hilarious, it's always entertaining, it's not particularly dangerous, and it's all Alaskan. You gotta love this place!

There has always been a bar on the shores of Lake Spenard. It started as a summer pavilion in the days of Joe Spenard himself and has continued with only short interruptions for changes of ownership, bankruptcies, and fires, both planned and unplanned. . . .

Mr. Whitekeys' Orchestra and Chorus was once hired

to play a benefit for the Anchorage Police Department so they could buy some K-9 Corps dogs. Except for the band, everybody there was a cop. The bartenders were cops. The waitresses were cops. The coat-check girls were cops. The doormen were cops. All the dancers and drinkers were cops. I brought my hot new girlfriend, and her brand-new expensive down coat was stolen from the coat-check room. Joe Spenard would have been proud.

WRITER RONALD CROWE notes that Anchorage boasts of having a downtown greenbelt called the Park Strip.

"Perhaps it does look more like James Watt's front lawn than a park, but it is certainly better than no greenbelt at all. Why, with no belt at all, the city's pants might fall down, and heaven knows what that might reveal. Spenard?" [4]

DURING THE REIGN of Governor Bill Egan, a violent ocean storm sent waves crashing over Nome's Front Street breakwater. The surging water smashed in the front wall and windows of several Nome businesses, including the famous and widely popular Board of Trade Saloon. Egan made a hurried visit to survey the damage.

As he stepped over the fallen wall and broken glass and peered inside the normally smoke-filled tavern, the governor observed: "The Board of Trade has never seen this much fresh air."

WORDS TO LIVE BY, from the wall of the men's room at the Elbow Room bar in Unalaska: "Live like Jesus did. Dance like Elvis did."[5]

Two miners were so sick and tired of each other, they drew
a line on the cabin floor and each had his own woodstove.

15 | Gold Fever

What a Rush!

Solitary miners have been known to improvise false teeth. One sourdough made a set of choppers with molars pulled from the mouths of a mountain sheep and a bear, then ate the bear with its own teeth.

A STORY TOLD BY writer Ron Wendt neatly captures the spirit and dogged optimism of Alaska's gold stampeders:

For Sawdust Pete, a prospector, the road had come to an end. While digging a shaft to bedrock one day, Sawdust Pete was killed in a mine cave-in.

Pete found himself standing at the pearly gates at heaven's door where St. Peter was keeping the gate.

Sawdust Pete started to walk through the gates. "Wait, wait, hold on there!" St. Peter said. "I've already got way too many prospectors here in heaven, and I surely can't squeeze another one in!"

Pete thought for a minute, then said to St. Peter: "You want to get rid of those other prospectors?"

"Well, yeah," said St. Peter. "But how you gonna do that?"

"You just give me an hour and I'll have all them prospectors outta here!" said Pete.

Within an hour St. Peter was shocked to see several thousand prospectors marching out the pearly gates. St. Peter watched in bewilderment as the grizzled miners filed on by him, flashing a grin now and then.

Not far behind comes old Sawdust Pete, just a grinnin' from ear to ear walking behind the throngs of money hungry miners.

"How in the world did you get all these prospectors out of heaven?" St. Peter asked.

"Well, it was simple," said Sawdust Pete. "I spread the rumor there was a big platinum strike in Hell!"

"Well, that's fine and dandy," said St. Peter. "But where are you going?"

"Well, you know," said Sawdust Pete, "I got to thinking about that rumor and there just might be some truth in it!" [1]

TWO SOURDOUGHS, sick and tired of each other, co-existed in a mining cabin divided with a line down the middle. Each even had his own woodstove. Tom and Jack went all winter without speaking to each other, but kept working by inventing a third party called Joe.

"Joe, tell Jack to crank up the windlass, the bucket is full," Tom would say.

Then spring arrived. Jack looked directly at Tom for the first time that year and said, "I'm going to town."

He was enjoying himself at the Monte Carlo with his

friends when Tom appeared. Tom asked if there was any-thing in Jack's end of the cabin that was valuable or that Jack cared about.

"What in the hell business is it of yours?" Jack asked.

Tom said he agreed with Jack, it was none of his business, but added, "I thought it only fair to tell you that before I left, I set fire to my end of the cabin." [2]

JOURNALIST RICHARD O'CONNOR described the gold rush machinations of a woman known only as Susie Bluenose, secretary at a mission at Golovin Bay, "a thirtyish spinster who always dressed in black and wore a stiff white shirtfront under her furs."

Susie Bluenose would show up at Nelly Page's road-house near Golovin, where she "assumed a position at the end of the bar and delivered temperance lectures."

She referred to Nelly's clientele as "sots," "tosspots," "rumhounds," "soaks," and "alcoholic wretches." While there may have been truth in some of her accusations, Nelly's customers also included many of the area's most upstanding citizens.

O'Connor wrote that "Nelly Page, realizing that she would soon be run out of business unless she took drastic measures, ordered her Indian boys to guard the door and lock it every time they saw Susie coming their way."

That worked splendidly until one night Rex Beach, the future novelist, his partner and two of the Seward Peninsula's principal guardians of the law, United States Commissioner Nudd and United States Marshal Lamont, dropped in for a drinking and singing session.

On this important occasion Nelly's sentinels fell

wrote "Iron Trail"

asleep at their post, and Susie managed to breach the defenses. She burst into the barroom and screamed, "Stop that music!" Rex Beach had been plinking away on his mandolin, but Nelly told him to play louder and continued dancing with Marshal Lamont.

Susie jumped up on a chair and shouted, "You blackguards, you roistering scoundrels, you're all going to roast in hell, do you know that?" She leaped off the chair and shouldered her way over to Nelly and grabbed the proprietress by the arm. "Young woman," she hissed, "if this racket is not stopped at once I'm going to have this den of iniquity closed immediately. I am going to report you to the United States Marshal!"

The music, singing and dancing stopped, and there was complete silence in the barroom.

Marshal Lamont disengaged himself from Nelly's arms, marched over to Susie and bowed gallantly.

"I am at your service, Madam," he said. "Would you care to dance?"

Susie fled into the night and never again interrupted the merriment at Nelly Page's. [3]

THE POEMS OF Robert Service are among the classics of northern humor and adventure. Service arrived in Canada's Yukon, just across the border from Alaska, in 1903, and was fascinated by gold rush lore and the bizarre characters who followed their dreams into the wilderness. He was a banker in Whitehorse and Dawson but quit the money trade to write full time. Service's rhythmic cadences and uniquely northern themes are shown to dramatic and startling effect in "The Cremation of Sam McGee."

The Cremation of Sam McGee
by Robert W. Service

There are strange things done in the midnight sun
By the men who moil for gold;
The Arctic trails have their secret tales
That would make your blood run cold;
The Northern Lights have seen queer sights,
But the queerest they ever did see
Was that night on the marge of Lake Lebarge
I cremated Sam McGee.

Now Sam McGee was from Tennessee,
where the cotton blooms and blows;
Why he left his home in the South to roam
'round the Pole, God only knows.
He was always cold but the land of gold
seemed to hold him like a spell;
Though he'd often say in his homely way
that he'd sooner live in Hell.

On a Christmas Day we were mushing our way
over the Dawson trail.
Talk of your cold! Through the parka's fold
it stabbed like a driven nail.
If our eyes we'd close, then the lashes froze
till sometimes we couldn't see,
It wasn't much fun, but the only one
to whimper was Sam McGee.

And that very night as we lay packed tight

in our robes beneath the snow,
And the dogs were fed, and the stars o'erhead
were dancing heel and toe,
He turned to me, and "Cap," says he,
"I'll cash in this trip, I guess;
And if I do, I'm asking that you
won't refuse my last request."
Well, he seemed so low that I couldn't say no;
then he says with a sort of moan,
"It's the cursed cold, and it's got right hold
till I'm chilled clean through to the bone;
Yet 'taint being dead—it's my awful dread
of the icy grave that pains;
So I want you to swear that, foul or fair,
you'll cremate my last remains."

A pal's last need is a thing to heed,
so I swore I would not fail;
And we started on at the streak of dawn
but God! he looked ghastly pale.
He crouched on the sleigh, and he raved all day
of his home in Tennessee;
And before nightfall a corpse was all
that was left of Sam McGee.

There wasn't a breath in that land of death,
and I hurried, horror-driven
With a corpse half hid that I couldn't get rid,
because of a promise given;
It was lashed to the sleigh, and it seemed to say,
"You may tax your brawn and brains,

But you promised true, and it's up to you
to cremate these last remains."

Now a promise made is a debt unpaid,
and the trail has its own stern code,
In the days to come, though my lips were dumb
in my heart how I cursed that load!
In the long, long night, by the lone firelight,
while the huskies, round in a ring,
Howled out their woes to the homeless snows—
Oh God, how I loathed the thing!

And every day that quiet clay
seemed to heavy and heavier grow;
And on I went, though the dogs were spent
and the grub was getting low.
The trail was bad, and I felt half mad,
but I swore I would not give in;
And I'd often sing to the hateful thing,
and it hearkened with a grin.

Till I came to the marge of Lake Lebarge,
and a derelict there lay;
It was jammed in the ice, but I saw in a trice
it was called the Alice May,
And I looked at it, and I thought a bit,
and I looked at my frozen chum;
Then "Here," said I, with a sudden cry, "is my cre-ma-
    tor-eum!"

Some planks I tore from the cabin floor

and I lit the boiler fire;
Some coal I found that was lying around,
and I heaped the fuel higher;
The flames just soared, and the furnace roared
such a blaze you seldom see,
And I burrowed a hole in the glowing coal,
and I stuffed in Sam McGee.

Then I made a hike, for I didn't like
to hear him sizzle so;
And the heavens scowled, and the huskies howled,
and the wind began to blow;
It was icy cold, but the hot sweat rolled
down my cheeks, and I don't know why;
And the greasy smoke in an inky cloak
went streaking down the sky.

I do not know how long in the snow
I wrestled with grisly fear;
But the stars came out and they danced about
ere again I ventured near;
I was sick with dread, but I bravely said,
"I'll just take a peep inside.
I guess he's cooked, and it's time I looked."
Then the door I opened wide.

And there sat Sam, looking cool and calm,
in the heart of the furnace roar;
And he wore a smile you could see a mile,
and he said, "Please close that door.
It's fine in here, but I greatly fear

you'll let in the cold and storm—
Since I left Plumtree, down in Tennessee,
it's the first time I've been warm."

There are strange things done in the midnight sun
By the men who mail for gold;
The Arctic trails have their secret tales
That would make your blood run cold;
The Northern Lights have seen queer sights,
But the queerest they ever did see
Was that night on the marge of Lake Lebarge
I cremated Sam McGee.

When liquor was prohibited in territorial days, "canned tomatoes" were known to taste amazingly like whiskey.

16 | Living in the Past

Schemers and Dreamers

of the Good Old Days

The town of Chicken, Alaska, was named by a group of miners who found it an excellent place to hunt ptarmigan. But they didn't know how to spell the word.

WHEN U.S. JUDGE James Wickersham first arrived in the territory in 1897, he was enchanted by the approach some of Alaska's people took to justice and religion, among other things. As in this story, related by author Evangeline Atwood: [1]

> While in Circle, Wickersham attended church services, which were held in the same room in which he held court on weekdays. He was fascinated by an incident which took place one Sunday morning during collection of the offering.
>
> Charley Claypool, a local attorney, was passing the collection plate and when he came to a young merchant, he stopped for several minutes, conversing with him in a low tone of voice. The next day the judge asked

Claypool about his extended conversation while taking up the offering and received the following explanation:

The young merchant put a five dollar gold piece on the plate, whereupon the deacon (Claypool) whispered "come again" and stood with arm and plate outstretched. . . .

"What do you want, you blackmailer?" asked the merchant, as he put another five dollars on the plate.

The deacon replied in a stage whisper: "I want the whole twenty-five dollars you beat me out of in the poker game last night," and remained waiting with outstretched plate in front of the young merchant's face.

Everybody in the church turned to see what had caused the delay. Blushing like an embarrassed school girl, the young merchant hastily took from his pocket an additional fifteen dollars and dropped it on the plate, whereupon the now smiling deacon passed on his way.

MANY EARLY ALASKA OFFICIALS were given to what author Evangeline Atwood calls "bibulosity." Describing the first officials sent by President Chester A. Arthur to establish a civil government for Alaska, she writes:

It was a motley crew who came north in the summer of 1884. It did not take long after their arrival to note that these officials shared a common weakness, namely an addiction to tippling. This state of bibulosity posed a serious problem in a district where "the sale, importation, and use of distilled liquors" were prohibited by federal law. It was conducive to a brevity of tenure.

Governor John Henry Kinkead was said to have brought with him an immense supply of cases labeled "canned tomatoes." The "tomatoes" were proclaimed as tasting exactly like Scotch whiskey and producing the same effect.

WHISKEY AND CHEWING TOBACCO got a good bit of the credit for construction of the Copper River & Northwestern Railway in the early twentieth century. "Problems, hard work and danger were constantly with the builders of the railroad," writes Lone E. Janson. "So much so that many felt that whiskey and snoose [chewing tobacco] were the only real comforts that construction work offered."

Only one labor strike was recorded during construction, and it was sparked by a shortage of snoose. Construction manager Michael J. Heney ended the snoose strike by rushing a freight car loaded with the stuff to the scene. [2]

NEWSPAPERMAN ELMER J. WHITE came to Alaska during the gold rush and became one of Skagway's two best-known residents, the other being con man Soapy Smith. These selections from White's columns—where he assumes the persona of the Stroller—give the flavor of his witty take on frontier life in Alaska: [3]

During the next several months Soapy Smith and the Stroller held services in Skagway, each in his own separate and distinct manner. Soapy operated with three shells and a small pea and used automatic artillery, while the Stroller conducted a mild-mannered newspaper in which he pointed out the rewards of upright living and urged his readers always to put a squirt of lemon in it.

Soapy worked on a cash basis while the Stroller extended credit, some of which is still extended.

The Stroller remembers that what little of the town he could see through the downpour was rather uninviting and he noticed that there seemed to be more paint on cheeks and lips than on buildings.

Bunks were a dollar a night in advance, with no extra charge for any livestock you might bring in with you. . . .

While the Stroller was at work on his hot cakes, an Irishman entered and was about to take a seat at the counter. Before he sat down he noticed a placard on the wall and he immediately turned and started for the door.

"That," said the Irishman, "is what druv me from home," and he pointed to the placard, which read: "Coffee Like Your Mother Used to Make."

There were dozens of other restaurants in Skagway during those days, but most of them were of a transitory nature and many of them changed owners oftener than the coffee grounds were emptied. . . . One restaurant . . . opened early one morning next door to the printing office and by mid-morning its proprietor had peddled enough hot cakes to buy a ticket to Seattle. He sold out to another fellow who kept it through the lunch hour, then sold it to a third party. The third owner served dinner, after which he got into a game of seven-up with one of his customers and lost the place.

At that time, in the first half of the year 1898, wives and children were scarce in Skagway and the result was that a great deal of affection was stored up to expend on them when they should finally arrive. Also, it was by no means uncommon for storage tanks to spring a leak, there being plenty of opportunity for acquiring punctures of that nature.

But by the middle of that summer every steamer came laden with women and children. When a steamer whistled in the bay it was not unusual to see two men carefully inspecting each other's coat sleeves and collars in quest of lingering hairs, for there was considerable wind in Skagway that summer, and hairs—red, blond and brunette—were wafted thither and thence by it and were likely to cling to any coat that happened by, and a great deal of trouble was saved by these careful pre-steamer inspections.

After the champagne had been flowing freely for a time, the atmosphere in the Pack Train became more exhilarating and some of the guests began to display talents the Stroller had not known they possessed and which they may not themselves have suspected. Little Egypt did a hoochy-coochy on a table and she—well, the Stroller cannot claim to be a connoisseur of the hoochy-coochy, but he has never seen one like it, and he noticed that the eyes of both Tony and Louie were close to popping from their heads. The Skim Milk Queen did cartwheels down the length of the counter but she over-estimated its length and a wheelbarrow was required to carry her to her boudoir in the attic over a butcher shop.

Nosey had one other quality, too, that was of great help to him behind the bar. He could look a woman straight in the eye and tell her he had not seen her husband for a week, and he could do this when the husband was at that moment crouching under the bar at Nosey's feet.

THE STROLLER ONCE WROTE about receiving a letter from a man who was looking for a bride. According to the Stroller, the lovelorn man wrote:

"It just occurred to me that you may know a woman there who is looking for a husband. And of course if she should happen to own a restaurant, too, that would be a good selling point as it would be cheaper for her to marry me than to hire a dishwasher. Be sure to call that to her attention. If I have to wash dishes, I want to stipulate that the woman is not to be over 50, but if she has money and I won't have to work I'm willing to stretch the limit ten years or so.

"Another thing you should impress upon her is that I am a man of simple habits. I have been living mostly on rabbits and sourdough pancakes and after twenty-three years of that a man is bound to have simple habits. Also, I am very thin. When I stand straight a line from the end of my nose to my toes misses my Adam's apple by less than a quarter inch but misses my waistline by nearly a foot. Find out if she wants me to bring my blankets. If she does, I'll have to wash them and as I have never done this I do not want to start now unless I am sure of coming."

RICHARD O'CONNOR WROTE of Skagway's Soapy Smith:

If one managed to survive the experience without being murdered, robbed, drugged, sandbagged, maimed or swindled, it must have been a delight and pleasure to meet Jefferson Randolph Smith. He had the fine manners of a Southern gentleman, the charm of a

Cagliostro, the persuasive powers of the devil himself. He was exceedingly chivalrous toward those weaker— if not at the same time richer—than their fellows. Women and children and stray dogs could turn to him confident of gentle treatment, especially if they did so in public. There was no doubt of his villainy, but he had certain saving graces, the wit inherent in most great swindlers, a sense of humor and a sardonic appreciation for the weaknesses of humanity. As he gracefully put it, "The way of the transgressor is hard—to quit."

"Go jump in the lake," turned out to be good advice to Susan Butcher. She did, and she raised $3,000.

17 | Howlers

The Truth about Alaskans

and Their Dogs

A dog musher needs two things: a wife and a truck.
And they both have to work.

ALASKANS LOVE THEIR DOGS. Tales of dogs and dog-mushing—and the lessons learned in the process—are enjoyed, repeated, and celebrated. Some samples: [1]

My dogs taught me to shut up and let them do their job. On one run, I talked to my leader Socks the whole time, and finally he laid down and wouldn't get up until I shut up.

—Kimarie Hanson, Anchorage.

Sprint racing is extremely addictive. Worse than cocaine and just as expensive.

—Don Hollingsworth, Seward.

I finally learned there are some things more important than dogs and the Iditarod.

—David Milne, introducing his date at the 1998 Iditarod mushers' banquet.

If you want to make your dreams come true, you must stay awake.

—Keith Kirkvold, Fairbanks.

Never eat orange slices with the same gloves you wear to feed the dogs their fish snacks.

—Linda Joy, Willow.

JOE REDINGTON, FOUNDER of the Iditarod Trail Sled Dog Race, encouraged the aspirations of Susan Butcher long before she became famous as a four-time winner of the event. Redington even told people that Butcher had star quality and would one day win the Iditarod. A friend cautioned Redington to tone down his predictions for fear people would think he didn't know what he was talking about.

"Redington, of course, always knew what he was talking about when it came to dogs and mushers," writes Lew Freedman.

He was just like a Hollywood scout or a football coach. He knew talent when he saw it.

Butcher was gung-ho to race the 1978 Iditarod, but she didn't have the money for the entry fee and supplies. Not surprisingly, Redington, who after all had managed to finance an entire race more than once, came up with a novel fund-raising scheme. He convinced Butcher that if she jumped into Knik Lake—after a hole was cut in the ice—the publicity would pay off.

"Joe said if I took a bath someone would sponsor me," said Butcher.

So Butcher mushed down to the lake wearing a bathing suit under a parka. She jumped in three times. And someone did sponsor her to the tune of $3,000. [2]

THE PEOPLE OF FLAT (population eight) really got into the spirit of the thousand-mile Iditarod race a few years back. They sold hot dogs to mushers and race officials, advertising the goods with a series of signs placed along the trail like the Burma Shave signs of times gone by: "After miles of mushing . . . Stop without rushing . . . Enjoy an Iditadog . . . The best hot dog in Iditarod."

JOE REDINGTON PERSUADED Channel 2 in Anchorage to come out and film a piece on him on Christmas Eve. It was another of Redington's schemes to generate publicity for the Iditarod race.

"The idea was that Redington would give an interview while standing on the back of the sled, then mush off over the horizon doing the Miss America wave," writes Lew Freedman.

Redington hooked up twenty-one dogs with Feets in lead. This was for show and Redington wanted to show well, but putting a full team in harness with no ballast was a mistake. At the Iditarod starting line a team of that size needs several handlers to keep it under control. An empty sled with only lightweight Joe to pull was a recipe for disaster.

Things began badly when Feets relieved himself on Redington's leg—on camera. An irked Redington shoved the dog away—on camera. The dog got even madder—on camera. So when it came time for Redington to yank the snow hook and give his little wave, he actually was barely holding on. Feets bolted from a starting position, exciting the team, and the dogs darted off the trail immediately.

For Redington, it was the equivalent of riding a bucking bronco. The dogs plowed through the ladies' camp [of Susan Butcher and Shelley Gill]. Butcher was in the tent and it collapsed on her and caught fire. She fought to escape the fallen tent. The razor-sharp snow hook bounced along. Redington hoped it would catch in the snow, only instead it merely bounced off of glare ice. Gill's Toyota Land Cruiser, complete with new tires, was parked nearby. The hook ricocheted off the ice and lodged in a rear tire, wrecking it.

The dogs swung wide and as they turned towards the trees, in a whiplash effect, the sled, with Redington on it, slammed into the vehicle. Redington was hurled off the sled as the dogs ran on. Covered with snow, he jumped up, climbed in his car and gunned the engine. Only he promptly stalled the vehicle in a drift. All of this took place on camera.

The well-intentioned Iditarod story turned into a slapstick comedy.

HERE'S GARRISON KEILLOR'S offbeat take on the Iditarod Trail Sled Dog Race:
We're going to Alaska to watch that big dog race,
a thousand miles to see who gets first place.
Those dogs are so handsome, tough as can be.
They don't complain and share their pain,
they're more well-bred than you and me.

PILOT TED MATTSON tells some good tales of the aviators who fly support missions for the famous Iditarod sled dog race. An event popular with the pilots is the annual

DR. ONEY FLIES REPORTERS IN.

Wet T-shirt Contest held in Nome on the night after the first musher crosses the finish line. Mattson was there:

> It's all in good fun, even if things tend to get a bit rowdy. When the town mayor vies for the job of master of ceremonies, you begin to see what long winters can do to folks in the far north. . . .
>
> How a stewardess from one of the Mark Air flights that landed at Nome that day got talked into entering the contest at the last moment by an Iditarod Air Force pilot leaves many questions unanswered. In any case, a costume was hurriedly assembled around her quite adequate features. What she lacked in professionalism, she more than made up for in beauty and innocence. Fortified at the last moment by two shots of Canadian Club, she timidly stepped up onto the stage. The front row went wild. A T-shirt and a pair of boxer shorts does little to cover up true innocence or a beauty that would have shown through even a flannel nightgown.
>
> You bid and pay big bucks to be a wielder of one of the water squirt bottles. It wasn't long before every contestant was dripping wet from head to foot. Cleverly cut T-shirts disguised little.
>
> Winners are selected by hand-clapping and cheering. The audience soon had it narrowed down to three finalists: a beautiful Native girl, a professional, and the boxer-clad flight attendant. In the front row, the trailbreakers and the pilots outdid themselves in support of their favorite. Miss Boxer Shorts won the $800. [3]

BOB ERNISSE, LONGTIME BARTENDER at Anchorage's Captain Cook Hotel, is such an avid duck hunter that he bought an expensive female Labrador retriever and hired a professional trainer to teach it the proper commands. On opening day of duck season, Bob and Anchorage engineer/politico Bob Bell loaded the dog into Bell's floatplane and headed for the Cook Inlet marshes.

They landed on a lake and within minutes Ernisse bagged the day's first bird. "Mark," he shouted, and the dog's eyes riveted on the fallen duck. "Fetch," Ernisse ordered, and the dog made a beeline for the bird.

The dog plunged into the lake up to its belly, then stopped, looked back at the two hunters and splashed straight back to shore. A frustrated Ernisse sent the dog back four times but each time it went up to its belly and turned back. By this time, Bell was bent over with laughter. "The dog can't swim," he shrieked.

Back at the Captain Cook, word spread quickly about Ernisse's non-swimming retriever. For a week his customers brought gifts to the bar, among them water wings and how-to-swim books. The dog later caught on and became a swimmer—but its humiliating reputation lingered for years.

JIMMY HUNTINGTON TELLS this story about his father, who came to Alaska in 1898 to find gold, married an Athabascan woman, and with her founded the Huntington dynasty of Indian traders and champion dog mushers.

One winter he was hauling a wealthy Easterner all the way to Nome. When they came to the shelter cabin the first night, Dad thought it would be nice to offer his passenger a little something besides fried beans, so he opened a can of fruit for dessert.

The Easterner looked at his tin plate with the remains of the beans still on it, then at the fruit, and finally said, "I would like to have a clean dish, please."

Dad didn't say a word. He just took the plate outside where one of the dogs licked it clean as a whistle. Then he brought it back in and everybody was happy, especially the dog. [4]

Notes

Chapter One

1. From the collection of Wayne Anthony Ross.
2. Story from Harry Yost.
3. By Judith Quinlan, in *Great Northern Lost Moose Catalogue*. Lost Moose Publishing, 1997.
4. From *Amazing Pipeline Stories*, by Dermot Cole. Epicenter Press, 1997.

Chapter Two

1. From *Fashion Means Your Fur Hat Is Dead*, by Mike Doogan. Epicenter Press, 1996.
2. *Outhouses of Alaska*, by Harry M. Walker. Epicenter Press, 1996.
3. Story by T. Ruth McCullough, in *Great Northern Lost Moose Catalogue*. Lost Moose Publishing, 1997.
4. From *Cry Not and Such Gems*, by Everett G. Gressley. Bear Paw Press, 1980.

Chapter Three

1. Story from Frank Baker.
2. From *Fairbanks: A Gold Rush Town That Beat the Odds*, by Dermot Cole. Epicenter Press, 1999.

Chapter Four

1. Story from Geoff Kennedy.
2. Story from Kellie McAnany, Anchorage.
3. From *Around the Yukon Stove*, by Mary Barry. MJP Barry, 1988.
4. From *Fishing for a Laugh*, by Lew Freedman. Epicenter Press, 1998.

Chapter Five

1. From *How to Speak Alaskan*, edited by Mike Doogan. Epicenter Press, 1993.
2. From *The Wit and Wisdom of Wally Hickel*, by Malcolm Roberts. Searchers Press, 1994.

Chapter Six

1. From *Fashion Means Your Fur Hat Is Dead*, by Mike Doogan. Epicenter Press, 1996.
2. From *Tales of Alaska's Bush Rat Governor*, by Jay Hammond. Epicenter Press, 1994.
3. From *Alaska Nicknames*, by Kathy Hunter. Lazy Mountain Press, 1988.
4. Story from Tom Jensen, Alaska Communications Systems.
5. From *Alaska Sportsman* magazine, June 1942.
6. From *Alaska Bear Tales*, by Larry Kaniut. Alaska Northwest Publishing Company, 1983.

7. From *Alaska Bear Tales,* by Larry Kaniut. Alaska Northwest Publishing Company, 1983.
8. From *Riding the Wild Side of Denali,* by Miki and Julie Collins. Epicenter Press, 1998.

Chapter Seven
1. Submitted by Tobin Brennan.
2. From *Tacos on the Tundra,* by Lyn Kidder. Bonaparte Books, 1996.
3. From *Alaska Nicknames,* by Kathy Hunter. Lazy Mountain Press, 1988.
4. Story from Geoff Kennedy.
5. From *Airwaves Over Alaska,* by Robin Ann Chlupach. Sammamish Press, 1992.
6. Used with Garrison Keillor's permission.

Chapter Eight
1. Story from Patricia Moore.
2. From *Amazing Pipeline Stories*, by Dermot Cole. Epicenter Press, 1997.
3. Story from Joanne McBride.
4. Story from Vicky Sterling.

Chapter Nine
1. From *Good Time Girls of the Alaska-Yukon Gold Rush,* by Lael Morgan. Epicenter Press, 1998.
2. From *Dolly's House: No. 24 Creek Street*, by June Allen. Tongass Publishing Company, 1976.

Chapter Ten
1. From *Alaska's Sky Follies: The Funny Side of Flying in the Far North,* by Joe Rychetnik. Epicenter Press, 1995.
2. From *Glacier Pilot,* by Beth Day. Holt Rinehart and Winston, 1957.
3. From *Glacier Pilot,* by Beth Day. Holt Rinehart and Winston, 1957.
4. From *Wager with the Wind,* by James Greiner. Rand McNally & Company, 1974.
5. Story from Beth Day.
6. From *Alaska's Sky Follies,* by Joe Rychetnik. Epicenter Press, 1995.
7. From *Alaska's Sky Follies,* by Joe Rychetnik. Epicenter Press, 1995.
8. From *Trails of an Alaska Game Warden,* by Ray Tremblay. Alaska Northwest Publishing Company, 1985.
9. From *Trails of an Alaska Game Warden,* by Ray Tremblay. Alaska Northwest Publishing Company, 1985.

Chapter Eleven
1. From *Bob Bartlett of Alaska,* by Claus Naske. University of Alaska Press, 1979.

2. From *Tales of Alaska's Bush Rat Governor,* by Jay Hammond. Epicenter Press, 1994.

Chapter Twelve

1. From a speech by John Hellenthal, reported by Russ Arnett in an article for the *Alaska Bar Rag.*

Chapter Thirteen

1. From Fishing for a Laugh, by Lew Freedman. Epicenter Press, 1998.
2. From Fishing for a Laugh, by Lew Freedman. Epicenter Press, 1998.
3. Item from Bob Fink, in Great Northern Lost Moose Catalogue. Lost Moose Publishing, 1997.

Chapter Fourteen

1. From *Amazing Pipeline Stories*, by Dermot Cole. Epicenter Press, 1997.
2. From *Mr. Whitekeys' Alaska Bizarre.* Alaska Northwest Books, 1995.
3. From *Mr. Whitekeys' Alaska Bizarre.* Alaska Northwest Books, 1995.
4. From *Crowe's Compleat Guide to Anchorage*, by Ronald Crowe. Sundog Press, 1979.
5. From Jim Paulin, Dutch Harbor.

Chapter Fifteen

1. From *Alaska Humor & Sourdough Tales & Other Oddities*, by Ron Wendt. Goldstream Publications, 1989.
2. From *Alaska Nicknames,* by Kathy Hunter, quoting a story by newspaper columnist E. J. White (The Stroller). Lazy Mountain Press, 1988.
3. From *High Jinks on the Klondike,* by Richard O'Connor. Bobbs-Merrill Company, 1954.

Chapter Sixteen

1. From *Frontier Politics: Alaska's James Wickersham*, by Evangeline Atwood. Binford & Mort, 1979.
2. From *The Copper Spike,* by Lone E. Janson. Alaska Northwest Publishing Company, 1975.
3. From *Tales of a Klondike Newsman,* by R. N. De Armond. Mitchell Press Limited, Vancouver, Canada, 1969.

Chapter Seventeen

1. From *Lessons My Sled Dog Taught Me,* by Tricia Brown. Epicenter Press, 1998.
2. From *Father of the Iditarod,* by Lew Freedman. Epicenter Press, 1999,
3. From *Adventures of the Iditarod Air Force,* by Ted Mattson. Epicenter Press, 1997.
4. From *On the Edge of Nowhere,* by Jimmy Huntington, as told to Lawrence Elliott. Crown Publishers, 1966.

About the Author

Tom Brennan was born on the East Coast. In 1967 he and his wife, Marnie, fled through the Rockies to Alaska, where they have lived ever since. Tom is a communications consultant, a former oilman and journalist, and a recovering fly fisherman.

 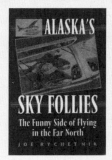